Soul Food

Encouraging Words for a Hungry Heart

Susan Weston Frisina

www.xulonpress.com

Dedication

In loving memory of my parents,
Everett D. Weston and Margaret L. Halstead.
It was his lifetime example of hard work and
her gift of encouragement that has given me the
determination to encourage others.

Foreword

When I met Susan, she was the most upbeat and encouraging person I had run across in a long time. She had been through some very difficult challenges in her young life, but she was extremely resilient. I learned later, through our dating relationship and subsequent marriage, that her relationship with Jesus Christ was a powerful and sustaining influence in her own external optimism, encouragement, and hope. I also discovered that the source of this relationship was rooted in the systematic study and devotion to God's Word, The Holy Bible.

Susan and I married within a year of our meeting. As most couples discover, even with a strong connection in faith and a shared relationship in Jesus Christ, marriage can bring some moments of conflict. Our newlywed conflict had a place of regular occurrence – grocery shopping. Susan was born and raised on the West Coast and I was born and raised on the East Coast. She was raised in a second generation Swedish home and I was raised in a second generation Italian home. Needless to say, our upbringings had diverse customs, cultures, and diets. As a new husband, I could be fairly accommodating to most of the custom and culture differences of "East meets West" with some of Susan's California tendencies. The one area I was virtually unwilling to accommodate was a change in diet.

This significant difference in culinary preferences made our grocery shopping quite a marital experience. We were so animated in our conflict that we discovered friends of ours actually coordinated their own shopping day to follow us around the store and be entertained by our demonstrative behavior. For example, Susan had a penchant for whole wheat bread. I was raised on white bread. Not only was there the matter of taste but wheat bread was about three times as expensive as white bread. Trying to strike a compromise, when Susan was off looking for avocados, I switched her regular brand of wheat bread for the four - for – a - dollar substitute. When she discovered my "trickery" she responded by telling me that the substitute brand had no significant nourishment value. In fact, she stated it was nothing more than white bread spray painted with brown dye. By the way, while I am receiving this education on diet and nutrition, she is throwing the substitute loafs of bread at me like footballs.

Over the years Susan has converted me to a more balanced and nutritional diet. I always attributed her efforts in helping me eat more responsibly on the California thing – fruits and nuts. I have to admit that Susan has been responsible in keeping me healthy, not only with calorie counting, trans-fats and cholesterol, but with the daily habit of feasting from the Word of God. You see, while it is very important to our physical health to be mindful of what we put into our bodies, it is just as necessary to be proactive and purposeful about what we put into our minds and what we digest in our souls.

In what you are about to read, Susan has compiled a daily diet of healthy spiritual food – food for your soul. A gifted story teller, Susan has transformed her ability to convey simple truths from God's Word into short stories that convey powerful spiritual life lessons. As you read each story, read them for fun and then for purposeful reflection. Look to identify the correlation between the metaphor and the spiritual truth conveyed with each accompanying passage of Scripture. Then ask yourself, "How does the truth of this simple story apply to my life?" Finally, look for how you can apply that truth to changing your own beliefs, thinking, and behavior to conform yourself into the nature and character of Jesus Christ.

In my own book, *Metamorphosis – Why Christians Don't Change*, I expose the fundamental flaw between what Christians know about Jesus and how little like Jesus professing Christians actually behave. In *Soul Food – Encouraging Words for a Hungry Heart*, Susan is able to create an emotional connection to spiritual truth that helps close the gap between knowing and doing. You will discover, as you close this gap in your own life, how your relationship with God, His Son Jesus Christ, and the Holy Spirit will explode with new meaning and purpose.

You were created to live a life that is pleasing to your heavenly Father. He desires your fellowship, your friendship, and your devotion. He will constantly pursue you, even to the depths of your own spiritual malnutrition and starvation to draw you back into this relationship with Him. So now is the time for me to ask you an important question, "How have you been eating lately?" Sweets and junk food rarely satisfy. The more you eat of them the more they create an insatiable lust that can never be satisfied. When you read God's Word, you receive all the nutrients necessary to change your life and live in harmony with the will of God.

"Your words were found, and I ate them, and Your word was to me the joy and rejoicing of my heart." Jeremiah 15:16

His word can be the joy of your heart and soul. *Soul Food* will make you laugh and make you cry. It will inspire you toward a deeper relationship with your loving heavenly Father. Read it slowly and with time for reflection. Read it to grow and read it to motivate you into the Word of God. The Holy Bible is food and nourishment for your aching heart. It is the only thing that will truly satisfy the hunger of your soul. What are you waiting for – eat hearty and God bless you.

Michael E. Frisina, Ph.D.
Senior Pastor
Calvary Chapel Northeast Columbia
Columbia, South Carolina

PREFACE

"A word appropriately spoken is like apples of gold
in settings of silver." Proverbs 25:11
The Holy Bible, NKJV

One of the benefits of having been an Army wife was that I have had the opportunity to travel from coast to coast. During these travels, I have met people from probably every culture group in our wonderful country. As diverse as these groups are, the one thing I seem to find lacking or in desperate need of in every case has been the need for encouraging words.

No story could describe this better than the day my six year old came home with the registration form for a 10K walk. He was filled with enthusiasm, and the promised medal to all who completed this run/walk drove him into the "begging mode" that afternoon. I had never even heard of a 10k walk until that day, much less participated in one.

The registration clearly stated that it was a parent and child event. The Army had my husband occupied (as usual) in a major training event so the responsibility to complete the form fell on me. Seeing the pleading face of my little boy I began to wonder how difficult this walk could actually be, since it was after all geared toward children. What I had not considered was that it was to take place at the United States

Military Academy at West Point, NY. This is a rocky, hilly place that reminds me of the hills in San Francisco. Naïve of what I was about to do, I signed the permission slip and went on with little thought about our upcoming 10k.

The day of the walk came with fairly good weather and what looked like the promise of a lovely event. This lovely walk soon became some kind of endurance test as we neared the half way point. My little one seemed to be still going strong and unaware that I was already tired and my get up and go had got up and went. It had been his bright spirit and joy that made me willing to participate in this event, yet it was suddenly not quite enough to keep me at it.

At this point, I began to notice people on the sides of road offering water, bandages, and small snacks to keep us all going strong. As nice and as needed as these items were, it was the encouraging words that these folks provided that kept me going. They said things like, "You are at past the half way point – keep going." Then you would hear, "You are going to make it," and other kind statements that seemed to fuel my desire to finish and keep my feet in forward motion.

At last we neared the finish line and there were even more encouragers standing to welcome us to the red tape. They stood cheering, clapping, and pointing to the finish line that would greet us as we both neared the bend in the path. These final meters were the hardest ones of the entire trip. We were both weary now, yet with those wonderful encouraging words we pressed on and we finished well.

My son got his medal! What a thrill it was to see that smile – priceless. It was so worthy of the effort he made to finish. Then my thoughts turned to those encouragers. Where were they now? What medal would they receive? Of course they were still back on the route, encouraging those who were still in the running, passing out more water, bandages, and words of encouragement to help keep the hearts and feet of the remaining participants in the race.

This is so like the race of life - not easy and not always turning out to be "just a lovely walk."

Sometimes there are blisters, trials, struggles, and other uncomfortable events that make up the crucibles of life. Yet these hardly compare to the lonely, hopeless, and despairing lives of those aching for encouraging words.

With this book, I hope to be one of the encouragers along the road in your life. As you read each short story you will find instruction, encouragement and living water from God's Word. I hope that each story will make you smile and give you the strength and determination to go one more mile as you press on to finish your own daily race. May you find it worthy of the effort and like the face of my little boy—priceless.

My very best wishes always and God's blessings,

Susan Weston Frisina
September 2009

Sound Off

Many of the men in my life have served, or are now currently serving in the United States Army. My father was in Burma serving during World War Two. My husband served as a career officer, both of our sons enlisted and served during the current hostilities along with a nephew who deployed to Iraq. Serving as an Army wife and mother, the military has been a major part of my life.

Army life begins with combat basic training. Our younger son did his basic training at Fort Benning, Georgia. Fort Benning is affectionately referred to as, "The Benning School for Boys."

Though not an official title, it is one that brings a smile to all who have completed their combat basic training there.

Basic training is hard work. Sweat, dirt, drill, long hours, and repetitive education on the fundamentals of combat. "We love it here, we love it here, we finally found a home," is a common refrain for any young soldier tempted to complain about the rigors of basic training.

The training is conducted under the watchful eyes of "The Drill Sergeant." Drill Sergeants are the guiding instructors, mentors, and coaches for these new recruits. Their primary purpose is to make sure these young soldiers learn the fundamentals of survival on the battlefield. This is serious business! This is hard work with long hours and requires a great deal of commitment and personal discipline! Any less of a commitment however, is to put every one of these basic trainees' lives at risk and minimize their opportunity for survival.

There is also basic training for the new Christian. Just like the soldier who learns what it means to be part of the United States Army, so too, the young Christian learns what it means to be a "Christian soldier." Hebrews 6:1-3 says:

"Therefore, leaving the discussion of elementary principles of Christ let us go on to perfection, not laying again the foundation of **repentance** from dead works and of **faith** toward God, of the doctrine (teaching) of **baptisms, of laying on of hands, of resurrection of the dead, and of eternal judgment.** This we will do if God permits."

There you have it. These are the basics of our Christian walk. Learning the basics and moving past the elementary elements of the faith. Without a firm understanding of these basics we cannot move forward in our walk as a believer anymore than a military soldier can advance to higher levels of individual training and development.

As a child I was always ready to graduate from one grade and enjoy the privileges and challenges of promotion to the next grade level. So too, in Christ, I look forward to the challenges and great privileges of ministry moving from one level of faith to an advanced level of faith.

Combat basic training forms the essential foundation for the future development and the skills of the military soldier. Your new life in Christ has begins the same way. There are foundational principles in the faith that will determine your success in future "battles" for the Lord. Now is the time to ensure you have mastered the basics. Singing to the tune of an Army cadence song:

Eternal life will make you glad,
Satan's lost and he is mad.
Warfare is awaiting you,
Time to teach you what to do!

Sound off!

Lost in Space

In 1965 there was a popular television program called "Lost in Space." Keeping with the theme of the decade, space exploration, the show focused on a family launched into outer space. Due to several mishaps they spend all the following years of that series trying to find a way back home.

My favorite character in this program was the nine-year-old boy named Will Robinson. Will was very much like the children's book character, Curious George. More than anything else, Will Robinson was constantly getting himself into trouble. Fortunately for Will, he had a robot that was always watching over him and trying to help Will with his self inflicted troubles. Whenever Will was about to enter into "real trouble," the robot would shout out, "Danger, Danger Will Robinson, Danger!"

We are all more like Will Robinson than we know or are willing to admit. We are prone to trouble, to getting lost, and to not knowing how to find our way home. Finding our way home, for Christians, means being reunited with God by putting our faith and trust in Jesus Christ. Through the mishap of original sin in the Garden of Eden by Adam, we all are separated from God. Unlike the television show, *Lost in Space*, we don't have to spend years wandering the galaxy before we find our way back home. Jesus said, "I am the way, the truth and the life. No man comes to the Father except through me" (John 14:6).

Once we receive Jesus as our personal Lord and Savior, we are reunited and reconnected to our Heavenly Father. Like the old song says, "I once was lost but now I am found." In the *Lost in Space* series, each family member had a job to fulfill to complete the mission and return to earth. While we live our lives, God also has a purpose for each one of us too. He has a divine plan specific to each one of us. You might even say we each have our own "mission control" in the person of God the Father.

With time, like most television shows, *Lost in Space* fizzled with the viewers and was taken off the air. Thankfully our lives will not fizzle as we put our faith in Jesus Christ. Our individual missions will be both a blessing to others and also fulfilling to us. This will lead us to the ultimate destination - heaven.

Now we find we have joy unspeakable in the "space" of time we are here.

That will leave us thankful to no longer be, "Lost in Space".

The Lava Field

In Hawaii there are many lava fields. The largest ones are on the big island of Hawaii. Lava is extremely destructive and leaves permanent formations of its past visits to the landscape. There are different names for lava formations in Hawaii. One of these formations is pahoehoe (pa hoi hoi). Pahoehoe forms as the lava cools and it is soft and smooth. Its physical appearance, in fact, is quite appealing in its own special way.

Another form of cooled lava is A,a (sounds like ah, ah). You can guess from the name that it is painful stuff. It is sharp and cutting and is one of the worst forms of lava in the world. A,a has a harsh and menacing appearance and it is hard to traverse.

The National Park Rangers knowing the dangers of A,a often put up boundary markers with warning signs not to enter these types of lava fields. In the history of these islands, enemies would strip an adversary naked and leave him in an A,a field as means of torture.

Psalm 25:7 says something about boundaries and torture too:

"Do not remember the sins of my youth, nor my transgressions; remember me, for your goodness sake, O Lord."

Sin and lava are so similar. Both are powerfully destructive and leave permanent scars of their visits into our lives. Thank God that Jesus has paid the price for ALL our sins and leads us out of the tortures of the fields of sin.

Transgression means to go beyond the boundaries. Park rangers put up warning tape to keep people safe while visiting the lava fields. Tourists who wander beyond the warning tape often suffer respiratory illness and some even succumb to the toxic gases and die. Transgressions are not slips, lapses or mistakes. Transgressions are willful choices to go where we have been told not to go. Transgressions are willful sins – just like A,a. Yet even our transgressions are covered by the blood of Jesus.

Our enemy, the devil, will often try to lead us back into the "lava fields" of sin from which God, in his love and mercy has delivered us. Only a true enemy would do such a terrible thing.

Seeing you now free of the sins of your past, your enemy, the devil, would like to take you back there and torture you with blame and shame. God has forgiven these sins and remembers them no more. So, neither are you allowed to go back into the memories of those fields either.

For goodness sake let's leave the past in the past.

It is only then that God can begin a much more impressive work – restoration.

Then the only fields of destruction to visit will be the ones left in Hawaii.

Who Do You Love

Sometimes when I have been around couples with very young children I have heard the question, "who do you love?" The child then responds with either saying or pointing to one parent or the other and everyone smiles enjoying the moment. I am smiling now just thinking about these same moments with my own children.

When I was a child, my mother taught me this poem:

I love me self,
I love me so,
I took me self to a picture show.
I sat me self upon me knee, then asked me self to marry me.
Ain't me cute?

(Author unknown)

When I came to Christ I decided I really didn't like that poem and its humor faded. I thought it was high time to replace it with something more along the lines of Biblical truth. So I wrote:

I loved me once,
I loved me so,
The love of God I did not know.

I thought of me self every day,
Until my life was in dismay.

Then I learned I had lived a life of sin,
And heaven could never let that lifestyle in,
So Jesus came to set me free,
to save me from a life of me.

I now love God and others too!
And dying to self is what I do.
I grow in Jesus every day,
As His Word illuminates my way.

Now doesn't that make you smile? Jesus said:

"You shall love the Lord your God with all your heart, with all your soul, and with all your might." Matthew 22:37

So, it is in choosing to love God first that we begin to find out what we are supposed to do with love. We were never intended to be in love with ourselves.

2 Thessalonians 1:3 says this:

"We are bound to thank God always for you, brethren, as it is fitting, because your faith grows exceedingly, and the **love of every one of you all abounds toward each other.**"

If you love yourself long enough - you will end up not liking yourself very much at all.

Love God. Love each other. Thank God for one another while you keep growing in faith together.

Now - Who do you love?

He Loves Me - He Loves Me Not

It's June and June is the month for weddings. I should know - my calendar is already filled with many weddings to attend. Every young girl dreams of being a bride. As wonderful as it is to be a bride - it is more important to know for sure that you are loved.

Today, while I was cutting my daisies, I was thinking of the way young girls like to sit and pluck petals reciting the verse, "he loves me, he loves me not" with the hope that when they have plucked off the last petal it would end on "he loves me."

Just like the bride hopes and longs for the love of her soon to be husband, so too, we Christians long for the assurance of knowing God's feelings toward us. While a young husband may falter in conveying his love to his young bride, without a doubt God has settled the question of His unending and unconditional love for us. In John 3:16 we read:

"For God so **loved** the world, that He gave His only begotten son. That whoever believes in Him would not perish but, have everlasting life."

Yes, I can stand on that sure word of God and know that it is true - He loves me!

But, do I love God? Think of Tevye in the musical classic, "Fiddler on the Roof," asking his wife of so many years, "Do you love me?" Now ask yourself – "Do you love God?"

How can we know that we love God? Sometimes we may feel that we love Him, but feelings ebb and flow like the ocean and are often changed by external circumstances we cannot control. Other times we just wish that we would love God, yet wishing something does not always make it so. Finally, when we come to the understanding of all God has done for us we have an even stronger desire to declare our own love for Him.

The Bible tells us how we can know for sure that we love God. John 14:23-24 states:

"Jesus answered and said to him, 'If anyone loves Me, he will keep My word; and My Father will Love him, and We will come to him and make Our home with him. He who does not love Me does not keep My words and the word which you hear is not Mine but the Father's who sent Me."

When we choose to obey and do what the Lord asks us to do, we know this is a demonstration and validation of our love for Him. If we continue to do our own thing and not obey Him, then He says we do not love Him.

After all, daisies are just daisies.

The "he loves me, he loves me not" while fun, is only a game. Today let's shift our focus to the one who made the daisies. Begin to live a life of obedience to show the world and tell The Lord how much we love Him.

Love and Marriage

L ove and marriage go together as the popular song says, "Like a horse and carriage." Seems strange to say that don't you think? The distinction is whether we mean love as a verb or love as a noun, and whether we mean love as emotion or the commitment to love for a life time.

Interesting how people who find themselves romantically connected do not have to be told to be relational – to make "date time." People who are in "love" want to be together and are nearly impossible to separate. In restaurants they gaze across the table at each other. The rest of us look on and we all know that they are in "love." Walking down the street, a couple hold hands and seem to smile without a care in the world. And the rest of us smile back because it is fun to see couples in "love."

Couples who are in love are endlessly interested in each other. Seeking to know and understand everything about the other person, we love to tell anyone who will listen about the one who has captured our heart. Inevitably, we marry and seal our love in vows of fidelity honored with a legal agreement.

Our relationship with Jesus begins just this way. The Bible tells us in 1 John 4:19 that, "We love Him, because He first loved us." We fell in love with Jesus. It was His love that drew us to repent of our sins and welcome Him into our hearts. We then became so interested in Him that we wanted to spend all our time with Him: reading our Bibles, going to Bible studies, going to church, and hanging out with our new found Christian friends. We would talk to Him praying all the time, and we would tell anyone who would listen about His wonderful love. Even the most cynical people around us acknowledged that something had changed in our lives.

With the passage of time, some couples who grow complacent and comfortable in the marriage begin to neglect their true love giving their attention and affection to other interests. Sometimes this happens to Christians in their relationship with Christ. We can sometimes go seeking after other things and our prayer life and Bible reading becomes more of an occasional chore rather than the joy of spending time with the one we love. Sharing our faith becomes uncomfortable and we may even decide that sharing faith is really a chore for someone else to do.

Couples who neglect the need to nurture their "love" relationship will soon have symptoms of marital disharmony. As the flame of emotional love begins to die down in this marriage, the legal agreement only serves as a reminder of the commitment that the couple made to each other. We start to do things because we know it is right to do them, not because we desire to be with the other person.

Christians who neglect their relationship with the Lord will also have symptoms of relational disharmony. Nonetheless, they will try and maintain what many consider a legal relationship with God. They will do the things they are supposed to do and feel secure in keeping a list of do's and don'ts in the "contract." Legal relationships can be burdensome and certainly lack an emotional element of joy. This is true for marriage and faith in Christ. It just isn't what it was meant to be without the relational connection.

The Bible tells us that the church at Ephesus started well. They had so many credits to their name in their works.

"Nevertheless," Jesus said, "I have this against you, that you have left your first love. Remember, therefore, from where you have fallen; repent and do the first works, or else I will come to you quickly and remove your lamp stand from its place unless you repent" (Rev. 2: 4-5).

Any couple can rekindle the flame of their relational love. All they need do is commit to spending time together and rediscover the joy and relationship that brought them together in the first place. Similarly, Christians can rekindle their lagging love for Jesus by turning around, getting back on course, and remembering the sweetness of their first love with Him. Time to start fanning those flames, don't you think?

We Will Leave the Light On

S ummer is a time for vacations, and vacations often mean a time of travel. As entertaining as a vacation can be, the time of travel can make you unravel. Summer is also the peak time for those in the hotel and resort industry to make their money. They draw their customers offering an understanding of how worn out their customers are from everyday life - not to mention the rigors of travel to the vacation destination. They offer all the comforts of home, and one even says that they will leave the light on for you!

One key factor in many advertising schemes is the promise of "peace and rest." Don't we all need rest? God rested. Did you know that? Let's go back to Genesis 2:2 where we read, "And on the seventh day God ended His work which He had done, and He rested on the seventh day from all His work which He had done." Now mind you that God was not tired, He was simply finished with creation.

A consistent question has been around about as long as creation itself, namely, "Will I go to heaven?" Indeed it is a very important question. In fact, not knowing the answer to that question can keep you up at night. It can steal your rest. Since death is going to visit every one of us, it is important to be ready for the trip and the final destination. It will not be a mere vacation from the hustle and bustle of this life. No, this trip must be well planned because your final destination will be permanent.

When Jesus died on the cross He said, "It is finished" (John 19:30).

The work of salvation was completed there on the cross. The blood of Jesus covered all the expenses for our leap from this life to the next. For the person who has put their faith in Jesus Christ - to trust in, rely on and cling to Him, you may enter into the rest of the finished work of Jesus. For those who have not yet prepared for the trip, Hebrews 4:7 says this:". . . Today, if you will hear His voice, do not harden your hearts." Today is the day of salvation for those who are willing to come to Jesus and then enter into His rest.

Jesus is the way, the truth, and the life. He waits for each of us to get tired enough of going our own way. He prepared the Way that we would no longer be harried and hassled by the cares of this world. Will you enter into His rest today? He is leaving the light on for you.

Jumping for Joy

A big promotion! The check is in the mail! You have won the lottery! A child has been born! You have found the love of your life. Are you jumping for joy? Each day so many good things are happening that we can easily forget to take the time to be thankful for them all.

In 1954, there was a song by Bing Crosby titled, "Count your Blessings." I just loved some of those words. "When you are weary and you can't sleep, count your blessings instead of sheep then you'll fall asleep counting your blessings."

In a day when anxiety is at near epidemic levels in America, when countless numbers of people are medicating themselves to cope with the stress of everyday life, I believe we need to sit down and do the math. We need to add up all the wonderful things God has done for us over the course of our lives. We won't just fall asleep knowing we are in His care.

We will find that the list is so long and the blessings so great that we could get tired trying to write them all down.

Philippians 4:4 states:

"Rejoice in The Lord always. And again I say rejoice."

Rejoice. God is at work in your most challenging circumstances. You are going to be amazed to see what He can do with your difficulties. God is good and He is so faithful! He desires to bring good things to pass your life.

Are you jumping yet?

The Benefit of a Broken Heart

A young lady told me the other day that she believed that we cannot recognize the benefits and blessings of love until we experience the sorrow of a broken heart. I can see how broken hearts can more easily become thankful hearts. Broken hearts know the loss of love and the pain of rejection. The question still remains — Is it really necessary to experience a broken heart to see the true benefit of love?

In our early days of marriage, my husband and I were stationed with the 101st Airborne Division at Fort Campbell, Kentucky. He was assigned to an air cavalry squadron. Their unit motto is "Out Front." These soldiers lived by that motto and "deployed" was their middle name. All the separations that Army deployments create can be quite a sorrowful time for a new bride adjusting as a new Army wife. The smart wives learn quickly that you cannot fight with Uncle Sam and accept the fact that deployments are a normal part of Army life.

Even with this acceptance, I hated to see my husband called out - never knowing when he might be returning home.

One day while reading my Bible, I learned that God allows everything for a good purpose (Romans 8:28). I began to invest my heart in the possibilities of what good purpose these deployments could bring to our home. With an open and broken heart, I was able to see that my husband and I grew to value each other more, knowing that what little time we had to spend with each other was precious. The deployments, though hard, were producing a good crop of thankfulness in our hearts and that was a good thing.

There is one other type of broken heart that seems absolutely necessary. Matthew 21:44 states: "And, whoever falls on this stone will be broken; but on whomever it falls, will it grind to powder."

Jesus is the stone referred to in this passage. I believe this is the necessary answer we are seeking. When we are willing to see that it was **our sins** that separated us from God and be willing to have our hearts broken - accepting the responsibility for our sins, we then are able to receive Christ's forgiveness and be reunited with the love relationship of all time. The Bible talks about our need to have a broken and contrite heart to come to repentance. In Christ, a broken heart is a good thing and leads us to a relationship with God that will last forever.

There are many people who are unwilling to fall upon that rock, confess their sins, die to their flesh desires, and discover life in Jesus Christ. Instead they proceed in their own strength and wait until that day when Jesus comes in power to judge the world. That day the stone will fall on them and they will be ruined for all time. Their ultimate problem is their unwillingness to come to the place of a broken heart.

As for earthly loves and losses,
And the benefits they bring,
I don't think love requires,
A broken heart to make them sing.

But, for heavenly love awaiting,
There is quite another cost.
It was for the debt we all have owed
That our savior bore the cross.

One love needs not suffer,
But the other is worthy of its pain.
For to be broken before ones Savior,
Is to receive the greatest gain.

All in all when you add it up, it seems that as hard as it is to have a broken heart, the benefits far outweigh the cost.

Tell Me another Story

C hildren love stories. I have enjoyed telling stories to
my own children, and I have also had the privilege of
sharing stories with my class at church. Whether in a formal
classroom setting or in the comfort of their little beds at
night, children love to hear just one more story.

I love the look upon the children's faces as the story line
develops and each character acts out in a scene. They seem
to be on the edge of their seats as the air is prickled with the
excitement of the stories they so love to hear.

This is just how Jesus taught to those who followed Him.
In those days, which seem so long ago, they called stories
parables. A parable is a story with the purpose of teaching
morals and principals. As we discover from the Bible, little
children are not the only ones who love stories. Mark 4:1-2
sets the following scene:

"And again He began to teach by the sea. And a great
multitude was gathered to Him, so that He got into a boat
and sat in it on the sea and the whole multitude was on the
land facing the sea. Then He taught them many things by
parables . . . ."

If today a good story teller can gather a crowd, the stories
Jesus told gathered a multitude! I can see them all upon the

land, young and old, children and adults, waiting in anticipation for Jesus to break the silence and feed their hungry spirits with another one of his stories. I wish I could have been a part of this multitude just to see and hear Jesus teach in this manner. With this desire, I am reminded that all those stories with all their lessons are still with us. The Bible holds the teachings of Jesus, written for us to read for ourselves and for those children who are open to hearing from The Master story teller.

One other thing about little children and stories is that they often have favorite ones they enjoy hearing over and over again. It does not matter how many times the story has been told. It does not even matter who is reading the story. They just love to hear the best stories over and over again. This is also true with the Word of God. You can never get enough of it. You can never know it all. Those words seem to have a life of their own that call you back to those oft turned pages.

My favorite story is the one that sums up the purpose of the Holy Spirit's inspiration for the writing of the Word of God. It truly is *The Greatest Story Ever Told*. It is the story of the love of our heavenly Father who gave everything to save His children from the bondage of slavery and destruction of sin. The cost of our sin was huge, but the depth of His love was bigger than the price of our sin. This story is written on every page, in every chapter, and every lesson of the Bible.

It is the story of all time.
That echo's in my heart and mind,
When I'm tired and needing sleep,
Or hungry when I rise to eat.
It's what I hear when off to work,
Or when I see the darkness lurk.

The story that I love so well
Is the one I so often ache to tell,
Of the Savior who gave all for me
Who covered my debt and set me free.

The story, that I always find,
The one that gives me peace of mind.
The pages that promote my rest,
It is the one I love the best.

This is when I bow to pray,
And my child like heart speaks out to say,
"Tell me that story again, Father."

Half Nelson

A dmiral Horatio Nelson is credited with creating the wrestling move known today as the "Nelson." There are various types of Nelson moves. Personally, I am most familiar with the "Half Nelson" that I became acquainted with in my youth.

My brothers were great fans of television wrestling shows during our early years. It was not all that entertaining to me, but it was either watch wrestling or watch no television at all. Consequently, I became aware of wrestling terminology and the application of wrestling moves.

The boys would first watch a match and then go looking to find someone to practice their new found knowledge on — guess who?

Yes, my understanding of these moves and how to get out of them deepened when I became their new opponent on our living room floor.

The "Half Nelson" can be a dilly of hold from which to escape! Your best hope is to avoid ever getting into the hold in the first place. Otherwise you are left at the mercy of your opponent, crying for help, and for me, hoping an adult was close by to come to my rescue.

The Gospel of Mark, chapter five, we find the story of a man wrestling for his earthy and eternal life as he battled with 1,000 demons. It is very clear that he didn't have the knowledge or ability to free himself. Much like me at the mercy of relentless brothers, he too was at the mercy of relentless tormentors. Beginning in verses 6-9 we read:

"When he saw Jesus from afar, he ran and worshiped Him. And he cried out with a loud voice and said "What have I to do with You, Jesus, Son of the Most High God? I implore You by God that You do not torment me." For He said to him, "Come out of the man, unclean spirit! Then He asked him "What is your name?" And he answered saying, "My name is Legion for we are many."

Oh, thank God for His abundant mercy! When we lack the ability or knowledge to free ourselves, we too can cry out to the Lord for deliverance. The question is whether you have spent enough time cultivating a relationship with Him so He will hear your cry. If it seems that He is a far off, it might well be that we have not kept close enough to the Master.

Finding ourselves in deep pain or sorrow, we usually discover our need for God. When we find that once again He is full of love and compassion, we also find that we cannot resist worshiping at His feet. Isn't it amazing that this poor fellow worshiped our Lord before Jesus set him free? That is the natural response to perfect love.

I was also thankful for a mother who loved me enough to respond to my cry, catch my brothers and save me from the torment of their wrestle mania. Though like the man in the story, I would struggle by myself at first, in desperation I would also cry out for the help that I could not do without.

God is more certain than mothers. He is as close to you as your own breath. His love for you is more than enough to set you free. He is only waiting to hear you give up on your own strength and submit to His plan and purpose for your life. And as for Admiral Nelson and the moves he developed - I understand he is now in heaven probably learning a few new moves from the Master.

Spring Planting

We are all familiar with the saying, "Spring showers bring May flowers." The seeds of the flowers we currently enjoy went into the ground long ago. Someone pulled the weeds, planted the seeds or bulbs, and came back (long before they could see any results) to fertilize the soil while the evidence of the resulting blooms lie still under the ground.

Galatians 6:7 says:

"Do not be deceived, God is not mocked; for whatever a man sows, that he will also reap."

The principle of sowing and reaping provides us many object lessons for living a productive and fruitful Christian life:

1. You will only get what you plant. There are never any special agreements with God that, in your case, you can sow one kind of seed and expect a different result at harvest time. If you plant corn seed you will harvest corn. If you sow pea seeds you will harvest peas. So, if you sow to your flesh you will get corruption (meaning

rotting decay). Look this word up if you want a more precise definition - just don't do it around lunch time.

2. By contrast, sowing to the Spirit does produce spiritual fruit in our lives. This wise principle can be followed by the saying *"Do not be weary in well doing."* In other words, "don't despair about those seeds that have not popped up yet." Gardening takes time. God's work will require patience, but the fruit will soon be evident in your life.

Do you want to live a productive, fruitful life in harmony with the Holy Spirit? Do you want a life of good things? Plant God's Word deep in the rich soil of your heart. Then cultivate it and fertilize it with Bible study, prayer, and fellowship. The alternative is a life in the flesh full of sorrow, pain, and the rotting fruit of a life seeking the failed promises of a lost and dying world.

When you want to ensure a healthy garden it pays to listen to the Master Gardner's advice.

You will reap what you sow – plant wisely, wait, watch, and you are sure to have a lovely harvest.

Finding Your Ministry

This is a common question in church today, "What is my purpose?" We all seem to have the same basic need to discover our meaning, value and purpose. For those of us in the Body of Christ we ask this question seeking to discover our ministry – where we can serve within the Church. Perhaps as important as discovering where to serve, we should answer the question of *why* we are seeking a ministry.

What is the purpose of ministry? Is it for personal fulfillment? Is it meeting a need to be needed? Is it to finally feel personal worth? Is it to build more churches, or possibly to enlarge a present on? Here is the answer from the Bible:

". . . and He Himself gave some to be apostles, prophets, evangelists, pastors and teachers, for the equipping of the saints for the work of the ministry. For the edifying of the body of Christ," (Eph. 4: 11-12).

Ah ha! God has given every one of us a gift of ministry. It is for the edifying (the building up) of the body (the members of the body of Christ). Though it is a blessing and a fulfillment to serve, the blessings is not directly in the serving as an end in itself. Nor is it in the building of the church - thought this too is a noble act of faithful service. And though while we in serving may find our need for a meaningful and useful purpose; this too is not the primary objective of our being equipped for ministry. The primary purpose of serving is to build up, to encourage, and establish our brothers and sisters in Christ.

So, it is very important that you seek The Father, find your gifting, and become a blessing in building up the people in your body. Not to satisfy your need but to fulfill God's plan for your life in Christ.

Amputation

After every war, unfortunately there are soldiers who return home with something missing.

The carnage of IEDs, improvised exploding devices, has contributed significantly to the number of American soldiers returning home with missing limbs.

It is common among amputees to experience pain from a phenomenon called, "false memory" syndrome. For those of us blessed enough to not know the pain of these injuries, we might find it hard to understand how something that does not exist can cause such pain. But, nonetheless, it does.

Still, we might understand this pain from our own experience in separation from God. While we do not have a physical attachment to our Heavenly Father, we certainly have known the pain of separation from Him. . We were separated from God by the original sin of Adam in the Garden of Eden. We continued in that separation by committing our own sins perpetuating the separation from God.

While we may not have known the source of this pain, it was real to us nonetheless. As the Holy Spirit began to work in our lives, we all felt that ache and loss to be back in relationship to the Father. From the beginning of time, we were made to have fellowship with God. To end this pain of separation all we need to do is acknowledge our condition, repent and submit to the Word of God, and we are restored in proper relationship with God.

Ephesians 2:14 says

"For He Himself is our peace, who has made both one and has broken down the middle wall of separation."

What separation you may ask? Why the separation from our Father who loves us and who we need so desperately in our lives? Jesus paid the price to reunite us with The Father. As the pain of an amputee subsides over time, your pain can end too. Today, receive or recommit to the free gift of eternal life in Jesus Christ. Let Him lead you from the pain of separation into the joy of the reunion in life with the Father.

Worn Out and Ready to Give Up

When you are exercising at the gym, the first repetitions with those weights are easy to complete. It will be the last ones, the ones where you strain, that really create the most benefit from your workout. Did you ever have a coach remind you, "No pain, and no gain?" All you could think about was finishing that last rep.

Like our workout experience, you will also have those moments of "no pain, no gain," in Christ.

In those moments, He is building your spiritual life with trials and difficulties to strengthen your spiritual muscles. The burden of these trials can make you wonder how much more you can endure. Like your coach encouraging you to push out one more rep, Jesus encourages you to keep going one more step in your walk of faith. When you do, you will discover the strength of our spiritual walk just like you discover the growth of your physical muscles.

It is in the pain of the exercise that the muscles break down so they can rebuild with greater strength. This is how we grow in faith too. The best investment in your spiritual walk is at those difficult times when you are at the end of your rope. The Holy Spirit works in you at these trying moments to grow and conform you into the image of Jesus Christ.

Ephesians 3:14-16 says:

"For this reason I bow my knees to the Father of our Lord Jesus Christ, from whom the whole family in heaven and earth is named, that *He would grant you, according to the riches of His glory, to be **strengthened with might through His Spirit in the inner man.***"

Our pressing on in Christ is no "self help" session or technique. It is simply Jesus doing a work in us, changing us, and strengthening us, not by our perspiration but by His inspiration.

Today, hang on, keep pressing on, bow your knees and ask Him to give you the strength. Then push out one more rep. After all, "No pain, no gain."

Power Outage

"There was a Jew named Apollos, a native of Alexandria, who came to Ephesus. He was a cultured and eloquent man, well versed and mighty in the Scriptures. He had been instructed in the way of the Lord, and burning with zeal, he spoke and taught diligently and accurately the things concerning Jesus, though he was acquainted *only with the baptism of John.*" Acts 18:24-25 (Italics added)

L et's get our facts straight about Apollos. The Bible says:

He was a Jew
He was well educated
He was a man of the Word
He was a teacher
He was saved
He was baptized
He was leading others

So far so good for Apollos and then we read in verse 26, "Aquila heard him teaching both fearlessly and boldly (Amplified Bible) and he and his wife took Apollos aside and expounded to him the way of God more accurately."

Interesting that given all we are told about Apollos, what more could he have needed to receive from Aquila and Priscilla? Stay tuned. In Acts 19:1, we discover that while Apollos was in Corinth, the apostle Paul traveled through the upper inland districts and came to Ephesus. There he found some disciples. These people were legitimate believers otherwise they would not have been called disciples. Then in 19:2, Paul asks them, "Did you receive the Holy Spirit when you believed on Jesus Christ?" And they said, "No, we have not even heard that there is a Holy Spirit."

We see again the confirmation that these people "believed on Jesus Christ." Note the use of the past tense – believed. So, they were Christians, yet these Christians had not heard that there was a Holy Spirit. Continuing in verse 3, "And he asked, 'Into what baptism then were you baptized?'" They answered, "Into John's baptism." Once again, so far so good. The first act of obedience following receiving Jesus is to be baptized. These were disciples, born again, and baptized in the baptism of water. So, to what baptism was Paul referring?

In verse 4 and 5, Paul said, "John baptized with the baptism of repentance, continually telling the people that they should believe in the one who was coming after him, that is, in Jesus. On hearing this they were baptized again in the name of the Lord Jesus."

Here comes the next baptism, "And as Paul laid his hands upon them, the Holy Spirit came on them and they spoke in tongues and prophesied" (verse 6).

The Holy Spirit is the third person of the Holy Trinity. He has personality and identity. The Holy Spirit is not some spiritual entity but completely God.

The evidence for the Holy Spirit begins in Genesis and functions as the powerhouse of the Holy Trinity. The Greek word is *dunamis* - this is where we get our word dynamic, and also dynamite! This is miraculous power.

Are you born again, baptized in water, burning with zeal, teaching and leading others to Christ?

There is more for you today! There is the miraculous power of the Holy Spirit! Perhaps you have been experiencing a power outage - power to change, power to overcome the world, the flesh and the devil? Today is your day to plug in and receive the baptism of the Holy Spirit. Simply pray to the Father to fill you with the total indwelling of the Holy Spirit and then ask the Holy Spirit to release His power, his *dunamis* through you. Doing so will continue your spiritual transformation into the nature and character of Jesus Christ.

A Prescription for Effective Relationships

Don't you just love those people who always have something good to say? It can be about other people or just life in general. Regardless, there are just some people who always have a positive focus regardless of the outward circumstances.

I knew just such a wonderful lady named Marie. She usually popped into the store where I was working during the times I needed a visit from a friend. Though I often saw her pushed and shoved aside by other customers, she never pushed back.

In fact she would say "Oh, I am sorry dear, am I in your way?"

At these moments I would think, "Hey Marie, they pushed you!"

But, Marie would only smile sweetly and wait.

When the rude customers were gone Marie would tell me that how we live life is too important to ever behave like that. Marie was a Christian and her life demonstrated the prescription for great relationships.

People like Marie are gentle, by nature, even when they have not been treated in a gentle way.

They wait patiently even when they have been kept waiting for a very long time. They like to come along side you and others and share your concerns, and they spread peace in the way others might spread icing on cake – with long, lavished strokes.

Hum-sounds like what a Christian is supposed to do - right?

Ephesians 4:1 states:

"I, therefore, the prisoner of the Lord beseech you to walk worthy of the calling with which you were called, with all lowliness and gentleness, with long suffering, bearing with one another in love, endeavoring to keep the unity of the Spirit in the bond of peace."

God help each one of us to be that person today. Help us to take the offenses and let them go. Help us to build bridges not to blow them up. Teach us and help us to be kind and gentle hearted even to those who are not kind to us. Help us to just be a witness for Christ - because He has done so much for us. Teach us to be obedient to your Word that it will work both for us and give others a dose of the prescription needed for healthy relationships.

Oh, Be Careful Little Mouth
What You Say

This is a little song from my days teaching children's church. So often I find that these little lessons are good for some of God's bigger children too.

Ephesians 4:25 states:

"Therefore, putting away lying, *let each one of you speak truth with his neighbor*, for we are members of one another."

Are you wondering why part of this verse is in italics? Well, the apostle Paul is quoting from Zechariah 8:16, "Speak each man the truth to his neighbor."

Now, whenever the Scriptures tell us anything, we should listen. But, when God starts repeating Himself, then we really need to listen. On this subject of truth telling, He repeats Himself over and over again.

I know that the subject of our speech and truth telling is not a very popular topic. Think of how many times you have seen someone in trouble for not being able to "speak the truth."

The Bible also tells us that Satan is the father of all lies. When we tell lies, the roots of these lies are in our flesh and the influence of the enemy.

Lies are like spider webs. They are sticky messes that ensnare and entrap us. Unable to escape the trap of the web we can even die in these lies. Let's remember, we are part of each other and need to tell each other the truth. There can be no trust in any relationship absence of truth in our words. Seems like I just read that somewhere before. How about you?

Litmus Test

There is a very strong warning in the following verse of Scripture.

"For this you know, that no fornicator, unclean person, nor covetous man who is an idolater, has any inheritance in the kingdom of Christ and God," (Ephesians 5:5).

If you are involved in sexual impurity, according to the Scriptures, you have no place or inheritance in the kingdom of Christ and God. After making this strong statement, the apostle Paul provides this additional warning, "Let no one deceive you with empty words."

In other words, don't allow others to tell you that disobedience to God in this area will not cause any great harm. Surely this wouldn't keep a nice person like you out of heaven – right?

In laboratories, chemists use litmus paper as a pH indicator to test materials for acidity. Blue litmus paper turns red under acidic conditions and red litmus paper turns blue under basic (i.e. alkaline) conditions. God has provided a litmus test for our lives touching us with His Word.

The Bible makes it very clear that if you really have a walk with God, you will stop living after the flesh. If you choose to continue to live a life after the flesh, don't be surprised if heaven's gates are closed to you.

What "color" is your life today, still scarlet as sin, or white as snow?

Don't you think it's time to find out whether you have an inheritance in the kingdom of God? What would God's litmus test show about your life?

An Example

The word, *example*, comes from the root word, sample. It really means to "in sample" or to taste. Immediately I think of the Scripture that says ". . . Oh, taste and see . . . ."

Philippians 1:27 states:

"Only let your conduct (behavior), be worthy of the gospel of Christ, so that whether I come and see you or am absent, I may hear of your affairs, that you stand fast in one spirit, with one mind *striving together for the faith of the gospel (the good news)."*

Every day you are preparing a feast for the world to see and sample as you put your life for Christ on display. This should be a life of unity and collaboration together with other Christians sharing the Good News. Once I had the privilege to visit the Culinary Institute in Hyde Park, New York. The Institute has large glass windows so that you may watch the chefs prepare amazing meals. Each chef has a stack of teaspoons used for sampling the preparations in the midst of the cooking process. Each chef only uses a sampling spoon one time. Each sample requires the use of a fresh spoon. One taste and in the sink the spoon goes. They continue the process until the meal has been completed.

Today I encourage you to pull out a spoon and take a sample of your life in Christ. Is your conduct worthy of the gospel of Jesus Christ? How was your taste test? Remember, if your life does not sample well with you, it most likely won't sample well to anyone else either.

True Gentleman

He who walks uprightly,
And works righteousness,
And speaks the truth in his heart;
³ He *who* does not backbite with his tongue,
Nor does evil to his neighbor,
Nor does he take up a reproach against his friend;
⁴ In whose eyes a vile person is despised,
But he honors those who fear the Lord;
He *who* swears to his own hurt and does not change;
⁵ He *who* does not put out his money at usury,
Nor does he take a bribe against the innocent.
He who does these *things* shall never be moved.
Psalm 15:2-5

Thomas Jefferson said that verse four was the mark of a true gentleman.

"He swears to his own hurt and does not change." In other words, a gentleman would be a man of his word. He makes a deal and later finds out he could have done better but still is true to his first commitment. Or perhaps you said you would meet someone (lunch for example) then a better opportunity comes along. Do you keep your original commitment?

Psalm 15 is packed with other good things we could stand to add to our character. For today, let's learn to be people who keep their word, as we develop the virtues of a Gentleman.

Under Inspection

"And this I pray, that your love may abound still more and more in knowledge and all discernment, that you may approve the things that are excellent, that you may be sincere and without offense until the day of Christ." Philippians 1:9-10

Sincere is a wonderful word. In Latin it means "to be honest, pure, genuine, and whole." In Greek the word *sincere* means "found pure when examined by the sun's light." Both meanings imply a sense of integrity, a wholeness and genuine nature of the article or person described.

In the ancient Greek culture, the word *sincere* was used in two ways:

1. When honey was sold it was either sincere or insincere. The honey was filtered over and over again until you could hold it up to the light and see that it really was pure and clean and ready for use. The purer the honey, the higher the price the seller received at the market. Less pure honey was sold at lower prices.

2. When carving a statue, the stone mason would occasionally slip with the chisel and nick a piece of the marble. To fix the imperfection, the mason would grind a piece of marble into powder and mix it with wax into a paste.

He would then take the mixture and fill in the nick and no one was the wiser. Except in the hot Italian sun, the wax would melt revealing the imperfection. Consequently in the market, you would see carvings advertised as sincere, meaning they were without wax.

It is really in the heat of difficult circumstances that our own integrity and character is exposed as to how much "wax" is covering our own imperfections. Anyone can act like Jesus when there is no pressure to be Christ like. Turn up the heat of the Son, in a difficult and challenging event and then see whether your conduct is sincere. Oh that we may be growing in knowledge, discernment, and love, passing His inspection of our character.

No Fishing Allowed

"Be kind one to another, tenderhearted forgiving each other, even as God for Jesus' sake has forgiven you." Ephesians 4:32

When I think of how freely and completely God has forgiven us and washed away our sins with His own blood, it reminds me of the way He wants me to forgive others. He has thrown our sins into the sea of forgetfulness to remember them no more. He does not want us to go looking for them once He has put them there either.

Psalm 103:12 says:

"As far as the East is from the West, so far has He removed our transgressions from us."

In light of how we have been forgiven, how good are we at forgiving others? As a young child, I heard the statement "oh, I will forgive, but I will never forget." Now that attitude is not forgiveness at all.

When I was a little girl, my family liked to go fishing. I do not remember ever encountering a "No Fishing" sign when we were out in deep waters of the ocean. I do believe that God has posted a "No Fishing" sign, however, in the deep sea of our sins. Once forgiven, there is no going back and holding past wrongs over someone's head. God has never done that to us and He expects us not to do it to one another.

Like all posted areas for "No Fishing," there are associated fines for those who break the rule. The Bible tells us that unless we forgive others that God will not forgive us. Go fishing in the sea of forgetfulness for past wrongs done to you and you will have to pay a fine as well.

So, today let's hang up the rod and hang on to each other.

With a heart of forgiveness we can choose to forget the past and help each other press on.

Father, May I

I have taught children's church for over thirty years. When time allows and the lesson is over, the children love to play a game. One of their favorites is "Mother May I?" Since we are in church, we have modified the name and call it "Father May I" to help the children remember to always pray before taking any steps.

The kids so enjoy moving forward, and sometimes I see cartwheels, crabwalks, and even normal straight steps while they play this little game. Regardless of the style, the children are always moving forward. It is amazing that they all want to be the first one to reach The Father.

". . . forgetting those things which are behind and reaching forward to those things which are ahead, I press forward toward the goal for the prize of the upward call of God in Christ Jesus."
Philippians 3:13-14

How funny that in all the times I have watched the children play, I have never seen a child look back during the game of "Father May I?" They are so focused on moving forward that it never seems to occur to them to look back and see who might be lagging behind. There is a lesson we older folks can learn from the children. How often are you tempted to take your focus off the objective, look backward to second guess yourself, see who is closing in on you, or even drop out of the game?

For the "bigger kids," we can be so tempted to look back at our mistakes or the mistakes of others and then lose our focus on The Father and our place in the race. Today would be a great day to say, "Father, I lay down my mistakes and also the mistakes of others. I am asking you to adjust my focus, and get me back in the game." Are you asking The Father to guide your steps and mark your path? Are you keeping your eyes forward toward the goal and the prize? I pray you follow the example of the apostle Paul, and press forward to the upward call of God in Christ Jesus in your life today.

Entropy

In a recent walk around my yard, I noticed some peeling paint on the house, a bunch of weeds in the bedding areas, and sections of the garden fence that needed mending. Inside the house, dust was resettling on end tables and book cases almost before the dust cloth was back in the pantry. On days like this, you really have to wonder how you are ever going to keep up with the natural law of entropy.

Entropy is one of the laws of thermodynamics. The scientific definition is akin to chaos - things moving from a higher state of order to a state of disorder. This definition is just a scientific way of saying that the things you work to put in order will naturally move to a state of disorder, disarray, and decay.

Did you know that this earth is passing away? The sun is cooling slightly every day. I am sure you have heard of global warming and other natural phenomena that supposedly are threatening the planet as we know it. Did you ever wonder where this law of entropy and process of disorder all began?

All the natural chaos and disorder of our planet began in a place of perfect order – The Garden of Eden. The Bible tells us that through the sin of one man, Adam, death and decay entered into the world. That which was perfect was now imperfect and corrupted. Try as hard as you might to retain "perfect" in this fallen world and eventually every-thing must submit to the law of entropy.

But, wait! I have good news from *The Letter to the Philippians*. All is not lost!

"Let your gentleness be known to all men.
The Lord is at hand." Philippians 4:5

Jesus, The Messiah, The Anointed One, The Savior, is coming again. The corruptness of the Earth, the disarray of our homes, and all the dust are signs of His impending return He promised centuries ago. That the coming is getting closer and closer. In fact, it could very well happen before you finish reading this sentence.

With that thought, what will He find you doing, thinking, and saying upon His return?

Oh, how I want Him to find me doing the work of the gospel! I long to hear those wonderful words:

"Well done thou good and faithful servant."

Are you ready for The Lord to come back today? Is there business yet undone in your life?

A personal relationship you need to restore? If there are things you need to put back in order before Jesus returns, do it today. He is almost here.

Family Squabbles

"As for the saints who are on the earth, they are the excellent ones, in who is all my delight." Psalm 16:3

"I am a companion of all who fear You, and those who keep Your precepts."
Psalm 119:63

Who is a Saint? The Bible says that we are beloved of God and called to be saints (Romans 1:7). So, now that we know we are loved and called saints, don't you think it is a good idea to know what a saint is?

A saint is one who has been set aside as a sanctuary for God and God's purposes. No longer living for ourselves we now are living a life in the employ of God.

It may be a joy to find out that you now qualify as a saint. While that new reality sinks in it is also good to realize that the members of your church are saints as well.

Now all saints might not be easy to get along with.

Some even seem something other than saintly.

This seems to have been a common problem within the characters of the Bible as well.

It has been said that the only thing that kept the people in the Ark and the stench of all that was aboard was the sound of the waves crashing on the outside of the boat.

Funny to think about, but we too have a flesh that has a stinking odor – a stench. Thank goodness God does not give up on us either. King David wrote that even in our worst state, we are all a delight to our heavenly Father. He even refers to us as his excellent ones.

So, stay in the boat you saint of God. Hang out with the sheep, and go beyond mere toleration but delight in them as well. Though we are not yet perfect we are all members of the same family.

Strong in the Broken Places

"That you may walk worthy of the Lord, fully pleasing Him, being fruitful in every good work and increasing in the knowledge of God; strengthened with all might, according to His power, for all patience and long-suffering with joy" (Colossians 1:10-11).

There is a little line in a song from the Disney movie "Cinderella." The song was "Impossible."

The main chorus of the song is, ". . . impossible, impossible, things are happening every day."

I really loved that line as a child. I still like it. As a Christian, I am often faced with my own sense of weakness, impatience, and a very stubborn and determined flesh. Quite frankly, there are days when living an authentic, Christian life, in the face of temptation, fears, and doubts seems almost impossible.

In fact, trying to live an authentic Christian life is impossible in my own strength. Thank goodness I am not alone in my own effort to make the impossible very possible. Have you ever looked at a piece of Origami paper work? It is amazing how a fragile piece of paper can be folded in just the right way and become quite strong in its fashioned form.

When God strengthens us with His power we become strong too. We develop patience, kindness, gentleness, goodness, and a host of other Godly attributes. Yes, we may feel weak in our flesh but He can do anything. The Bible tells us, "I can do all things through Christ who strengthens me" (Philippians 4:13).

Today, don't let the enemy tell you that you are hopeless, or point out your faults and tell you that you are not strong enough to resist temptation and endure trials. To overcome these strongholds in your life, you have the limitless power of God on your side! Impossible you say? No Way! He has made you strong in your broken places.

Out of Order

One day, while waiting in line at a gas station, I finally reached the pump only to find an "Out of Order" sign taped to the nozzle. What a frustration. I needed gas. I had been in line to use that pump. My only recourse was to get in another line and wait again for another pump to fill my gas tank.

Colossians 1:18 says this:

"He is the head of the body, the church, who is the beginning, the first born from the dead, that in <u>all things</u> He may have the preeminence."

It is such a thrill to hear so many in our church body say how they truly desire to experience God's will and plan for their lives. That they want to be empowered, improved and employed in the work of God. Yet, so often like that gas pump I encountered, things are "Out of Order."

Here in Colossians we learn that Jesus is the head of our body. He is the top, the one who should be in control, and **everything** should be submitted to Him. The last line sums it up, "that in ALL things He may have the preeminence." That is a long way of saying in everything He comes first.

When Jesus is in control, when He is first, our little pumps are ready for use. Oh, how sad I would be for the Lord to choose another pump for His service and pass me by because I was "Out of Order."

It has been said, "The world is still waiting to see what God will and can do with a man (or woman) who is totally submitted to Him." Today, let's throw out the "Out of Order" sign.

This little pump is open for God's business, how about you?

Dress Code

During the years we served in the Army, our entire family was very aware of the military dress code. This dress code was not only for military members, but also the members of the military family. Special events imposed not only uniforms but, acceptable dress for those who accompanied those events. There were even clothing specifications in place to let us know what was required to be worn when mowing the lawn or even shopping at the local exchange.

A military uniform is uniquely designed and decorated for a specific purpose. There are a number of combinations of shirts, trousers, and jackets. Every detail of that uniform identified the members unit, rank, branch specialty, and any special training schools. Could it be that God has also established a "dress code" for those of us who have come to live for Jesus?

Colossians 3:8-9 says this:

"But now you yourselves are to put off all these: *anger, wrath, malice, blasphemy, filthy language out of your mouth, do not lie one to another,* since you have put off the old man with his deeds."

In the Army, a new recruit steps off the bus and is marched to the barber to put off an inappropriate hair style. From the barber shop a recruit receives a full array of uniforms. This is the time of the putting off of the old and putting on with the new identity of being "in the Army." So too in Christ, we are to put off the old things from an old way of life and put on "the new."

Thank God it does not stop there! Next comes learning how to make a bed, how to march, and how to acknowledge superiors with salutes and appropriate verbal responses.

Colossians 3:12-13 does just that for the soldiers of the cross:

". . . put on *tender mercies, kindness, humility, meekness, long-suffering;*
Bearing with one another, and forgiving one another, if anyone has a complaint against another; even as Christ forgave you, so you must do."

Maybe today is a good day to look into the mirror and check out your uniform. Adjusting to the new dress code will help you become the representation of the message your want to send to a lost and hurting world.

It may be then that you experience that unseen, but silently felt salute from heaven from a very pleased heavenly Father.

The Slave and His Master

At the outset, the title for today's reading might be a turn off.

After all, the word slave or master has the ability to shake us up a bit.

At the time of Christ, nearly two-thirds of the known world's population was in some form of slavery. There were many different levels of slavery. Slavery was composed of everything from domestic servants to what could look remarkably similar to today's modern employee.

Bond servants were servants by choice and were considered part of the families for whom they worked. Other categories of slaves were non-voluntary. They became servants by birth, through spoils of war, or by failing to pay off debt. Historically, all types of slavery had term limits. So, at the end of the term, servants had the choice of either finding other employment or they could choose to continue with their masters voluntarily.

Which brings us to our scripture for today? Colossians 3:22-23 states:

"Bondservants, obey in all things your masters according to the flesh, not with eye service, as men-pleasers, but, in sincerity of heart, fearing God. And, whatever you do, do it heartily, as to the Lord and not to men."

Notice there is no escape clause in this verse. We know that Paul was not advocating that slaves run away from their masters. Slaves who tried to escape could be immediately put to death. These were harsh and cruel times. Paul is providing advice for how slaves were to represent their faith to their masters.

Note what is missing from this passage. It does not say "unless you don't like the way things are being run." Remember, you are not the boss. It does not say "unless you don't like your boss."

It does not say "unless you think you deserve more money for the job." You probably agreed to work for the wages you are getting.

This passage does say "obey." God is watching! Whenever we are working (either at home or in the work place) we are working for God. So, do it heartily for Him and not for promotion or praise. Working can even be considered your ministry.

Today, if you are a homemaker, self-employed or work for someone else, the manner in which you work will be your witness for Christ.

Cause me Master to obey
To represent You in the way
I daily work and then display
My service Lord for You.

Catch & Release

For those of you who are avid fishermen, you will already know about "catch & release" programs. For those less knowledgeable of fishing terms, "catch and release" is when fishermen must return their catch to the water. Though they catch the fish, they do not take them home for dinner. Instead they must release the fish to be caught another day.

Psalm 17:4 says:

"Concerning the works of men,
By the word of your lips I have kept away from the paths of the destroyer."

Our enemy, the devil, is nothing like the fishermen who comply with "catch and release" programs. At first the enemy will flash the lure to draw you into a behavior and have you think, "ah, this won't hurt me." Then before you know it, the behavior has you hooked.

The enemy (whom the Lord tells us is lawless) does not comply with "catch and release" laws. The poor person is hooked though they may squirm and splash about.

Fortunately, the Bible says that whom the Son sets free is free indeed. You have the power to break away in the power of God's grace. It is certain that the devil is not your friend no matter how tempting the bait looks.

Today be like David and say, "I have kept away from the paths of the destroyer."

And instead of being on the wrong side of the hook – may you now find yourself

A Fisher of men.

Splish, Splash

Colossians 2:12 states, ". . . buried with Him in baptism in which you were also raised with Him through faith in the working of God, who raised Him from the dead."

Jesus was baptized by John in the Jordan. We are told over and over in the New Testament to repent and be baptized. The Greek word for baptism is *baptizo*. It means to cover fully with a fluid, or to wash. The church at Colossae was a new work. They had received Christ and had taken the first act of obedience following salvation which is to be baptized.

Now, here we are in Colossians and Paul is teaching them again about baptism. Baptism does not save, but it is a physical, public act of obedience. It testifies that we have died to ourselves and our old ways and now by faith we rise from that baptismal pool to a new life. Just as Jesus was raised from the dead, now we live a new life too. That life is the new life in Christ.

Though one hundred baptisms will not save, baptism is still very important.

It says I am going to now live for Jesus. If you have repented from your sins and accepted Christ, then baptism is the next step for you.

Come on in — the water's fine!

The Little Big Horn

I believe that every American child knows the story of General Custer and the battle at the Little Big Horn. During our years at West Point, I often visited the grave of General Custer and his wife. Every visit provoked thoughts of his final battle. I wondered what the last moments of his life must have been like. At the end, General Custer, in the company of his brother and a few soldiers were completely encircled by entire Sioux nation. Do you ever feel like Custer, completely surrounded by your enemies? I know many times I have had this feeling of total helplessness.

Psalms 18:3-4, says something wonderful.

"I will call upon The Lord, who is worthy to be praised, so shall I be saved from my enemies.
The pangs of death encircled me and the floods of ungodliness made me afraid."

Wow, sometimes I do feel surrounded. The enemy seems relentless, but Jesus has already fought the final battle so that I will not have to. It is in these trying times, and shall I admit, terrifying moments that I call on my Lord. He is so worthy to be praised because I can recall all the other times He has come through for me. I then remember that He will also win this current battle – He always does!

It won't matter that I am out gunned, out manned or just plain worn out. It won't even matter that I am afraid. He is a come through God. Shh.....if you are very quiet I bet you can hear the cavalry coming to your aid.

A Band of Brothers

Invincible — do you ever feel invincible? I cannot understand why some people would choose to go it alone when they can instead have a band of brothers (or sisters). No one really ever succeeds alone. We all need someone to share the load, someone to laugh with, and someone to cry with, and even someone to minister to our wounds as we also minister to others.

Paul, the apostle, seems to be a person who was invincible. Though he was stoned – he survived.

Though he was beaten he recovered. And even when his enemies sought his live, it was his brother's in Christ who let him down the walls of the city in a basket to make his escape.

Paul stayed connected to his band of brothers until the very end of his life and ministry.

Colossians 4:7 tells us about one of those brothers. "Tychicus, a beloved brother, faithful minister, and fellow servant in The Lord, will tell you all the news about me.

And we learn of others in verses 9-14. Onesimus was a faithful and beloved brother. Aristarchus was a fellow prisoner. Mark and Jesus who is called Justus, fellow workers for the kingdom of God who were of the circumcision; they have proved to be a comfort to me. Epaphras, a bondservant of Christ, labored fervently in prayers. Then there was Luke, the physician, and Demas.

Even when Paul was at the end of his life he was surrounded by a band of brothers ministering to his needs.

Shakespeare wrote, "we few, we merry few, we band of brothers" (Henry the V).

We too are banded together in the love of Christ. Love for Him and love for each other. We each need the gifting of those who share our faith. No one person or gift more important than the other. No one - not even our hero Paul was able to go it alone.

The enemy may tell you that you are stronger, better, or wiser. Don't you believe it!

It is the trap of pride that will destroy you.

Get back to your band of brothers and march on to victory in Christ.

At a Loss for Words

Even for people who love to talk, there will be those times when they are at a complete loss for words to suit an occasion. Sometimes, it is during a time of such depth of joy that words just can't measure up to express our feelings. At other times it is during the grief and loss of someone we love. Whenever you find yourself in one of these situations, I encourage you to refer to Thessalonians.

Some of the dear members of the church in Thessalonica had died. A time of grief had set in among its members. Grief always seems to stir up questions - even for those most grounded in their faith. Paul said in I Thessalonians 4:18, "Wherefore, comfort one another with these words." What words? Wherefore refers to the words preceding 4:18.

"But, I would not have you to be ignorant, brethren, concerning them which are asleep, that ye sorrow not, even as others which have no hope. For if we believe that Jesus died and rose again, even so them also which are asleep in Jesus will God bring with Him. For this we say unto you by the word of the Lord, that we which are alive and remain unto the coming of the Lord shall not prevent them which are asleep. **For the Lord himself shall descend from heaven with a shout, with the voice of the archangel, and with the trump of God: and the dead in Christ shall rise first.**

Then we which are alive and remain shall be caught up together with them in the clouds, to meet the Lord in the air. And so shall we ever be with the Lord!"

Asleep is a euphemism for death. So, when exactly does the person who has died go to be with Jesus? Well, we just read that it is prior to us who remain - right? But, where are they now?

2 Corinthians 5:8 answers that question, ". . . for to be absent from this body is to be present with the Lord." In the moment we die we leave this body behind. Then we become present with the Lord. So, our loved ones who have died are in the presence of our Lord. The Bible tells us that, "In His presence is fullness of joy." While we may be at a loss of words in our grief, we can be encouraged and have confidence that our loved ones are experiencing a joy unspeakable and full of glory.

How Can I Find Joy

Everywhere I look, I see people today seeking to find a few moments of joy in their daily lives.

Commercial television and newspaper ads bombard us with enticements to joy and happiness. Employers are encouraged to conduct employee satisfaction surveys to discover how to make their employees "happy."

Chara, is the Greek word for *joy*. It literally means *to cheer or delight*. If you have seen the movie, "Chronicles of Narnia" it was the Turkish delight that lured young Edmond into the trap of the White Witch. His uncontrollable desire for the candy ultimately leads to the betrayal of his brother and sisters. So, seeking to indulge our flesh appetites with delight is not the most effective way to live a joyful life.

Often it is the case that people pursue joy as an end in and of itself. When you ask people why they want money, they can respond to buy things. When you ask them why they want to buy things, they can respond to make them feel good – for the pleasure. Yet, we know that sort of enjoyment is so short lived.

When our little Grandson looks up at me with those big, blue eyes of his, I am awash with joy. It is the end product of the relationship I have with him. Even when I am not able to be with him the sweet memories of that little one make me smile over and over again.

Paul said in 1Thessalonians 2:20, referring to the believers, *"You are our glory and joy."* It was seeing the faces of those in the faith who were growing and serving each other in the body that gave him joy. Many years ago I heard someone say that joy was "Jesus, others and then self". I thought about that quotation over and over again, and as good as it is, it still doesn't quite do it for me.

Ultimately, the source of joy is Jesus. Joy is a product of living a life in harmony with the Word of God. That does not mean you will never have difficulties. What it means is that your joy is not dependent on your circumstances but on your relationship with Jesus.

We like my grandson bring great joy to Jesus, and Jesus like the Grandparent looks down with a heart that is full of love.

This experience results in overflowing, never ending, always extending joy!

The Questions

It appears that every culture has a similar question that demands an answer – "What is truth?"

The Greeks, for example, with their philosophers, spent a great deal of time in pursuit of the answer to the question, "What is truth?" If we considered the prevailing question of the American culture it might be a different question – "What is good?"

Since the 1960's, moral relativism has dominated the moral thinking of America. The idea behind moral relativism is that there is no absolute truth. This flawed concept has left most Americans stumbling in the dark like some drunken sailor. It is time we settle the question, not only for ourselves, but for all those who are seeking now and who will come after our generation.

What is good? The Bible says, "God is good." How do I know? Jesus said so. In Matthew 19:17, Jesus said, ". . . no one is good but One that is God . . . ." *Good* is not some measuring stick. *Good* is not a set of weights and measures we try to balance between good choices and bad choices. In the Greek language, the word *good* simply means to be pure, beautiful, virtuous, valuable, and honest. No wonder only God is good.

So, how shall we find our way home to the Truth?

Micah 6:8 says, "He has shown you, O man, what is good; and what does the LORD require of you? But to do justly, to love mercy, and to walk humbly with your God."

We need to look no further than the daily news to see the need for justice. Justice is just the process of doing what we know to be right. How can America ever know what is right unless we agree together to hold a common standard of righteousness?

In the formation of our country that standard was the Bible. Once justice is in place we need to employ mercy to the situations that fall before us. Mercy is the gift of receiving what you have not earned. Mercy is never the check you are owed. No, it is the undeserved offering bestowed by a kind and tender heart.

What is the hope for America if not the need to seek some humility?

Humility is the act of willing submission to the authority placed over us.

Of course that submission begins at the foot of the cross.

Jesus said, "I am the way, **the truth** and the life. No man comes unto the Father but, by me," John 14:6.

Question answered?

The dye now cast,

The quest for truth is found at last!

God Did It

"The heavens declare the glory of God; And the firmament shows His handiwork. Day unto day utters speech, and night unto night reveals knowledge. There is no speech or language where their voice is not heard" Psalm 19:1-3.

Creation is speaking in a way that the whole world can both see and understand the message it is sending. So, what is the message? Creation is speaking of its Creator, of its awesome wonder.

When you read Psalm 19, you will find it talks about the sun and its courses. The sun, which is the perfect distance from the earth, sustains creation. The sun alone is an awesome element of creation. Even so, without the boundaries of its course - life on Earth could not be sustained.

Years ago, when I was in a school science classes, we studied about the "simple cell."

Well, it turns out the simple cell is really not very simple at all. The cell defends itself, recreates itself, and its complexity is still the basis for continuing research and development.

Yes, the message that creation is sending us is that there is a God. Sooner or later everyone everywhere will have to grapple with that message. With so much evidence for God in creation, why do so many people still choose not to believe? We find the answer again by turning to the Word.

"For everyone practicing evil hates the light and does not come to the light, lest his deeds should be exposed" John 3:20.

It is not about the great intellectual arguments. It is not about a lack of evidence. We are surrounded by a mountain of evidence. It is unwillingness for exposure, accountability and responsibility for our behavior that pulls mankind back away from the knowledge of God.

I believe that people who are practicing evil are miserable. Just watch them the day after they have had too much to drink. Did you ever stop to think that the inside of a toilet bowl was never created for a person's head? Rich or poor that bowl looks the same and serves the same need on the morning after too much libation. Yet, they both consider the event that drove them to the "bowl" fun. Let's be reasonable.

Who made the world? God did that's who! He is our Creator and He loves us. His creation is declaring to us His glory. Today, sit back, take in His handiwork, and enjoy His presence, and leave the "bowl" for its original creation.

Please and Thank You

I just love to go to Chic-fil-A. Not only is it a good source of fast food, but you even get a serving of manners on the side! I don't know how they established their customer service standards, but I can think of many businesses that need to take a few lessons from the "Eat More Chicken" folks.

The effect of the words "please" or "thank you" can have such a big impact on us as customers. This being the case, how can the word *please* impact us as Christians in our daily walk?

The Greek word for *please* is "aresko." The meaning might surprise you. It means to be agreeable. In business, there is that old adage, "the customer is always right." If you are in business, you know this to be true even when the customer is wrong. Part of what is required to stay in business is to be agreeable – especially with your customers. A good lesson for Christians to learn is to be agreeable.

1 Thessalonians 4:1 says, ". . . that you should abound more and more, just as you received from us how you ought to walk and to please God."

We have been called to come into agreement with God, agreement with His word concerning our behavior, agreement with His word concerning grace, love, forgive-ness, and our relationship with Him. We go on to read:

"For you know what commandments we gave you through the Lord Jesus.
For this is the will of God your sanctification; that you abstain from sexual immorality; that each of you should know how to possess (control) his own body in purity and honor. Not to be used in the passions of lust like the heathen who are ignorant of the true God and have no knowledge of His will. That no man transgresses and overreaches his brother and defrauds him in this matter or defraud him in business. For the Lord is an avenger in all these things."

So, just like pleasing or agreeing with customers which is imperative in business,
It is more important that we please/agree with God in our daily living. As I drive out of "Chic fil A," I always say "Thank you." And I hear those words back every time, "It's my pleasure to serve you."
Oh, that today we would together in one great chorus say to The Lord "thank you Father, it is my pleasure to agree with you and to serve you!

Moving Day

Today, while working in my garden, I decided to finally move a hydrangea. Though it was growing, it was in the wrong soil and wrong location for it to thrive and really make those lovely hydrangea flowers that are so attractive. Even though it was in the wrong location, it was still able to get well rooted. Moving day for this plant was quite an ordeal. I had to break up the hard ground around the root bed. Then I had to carefully work the plant out of the ground, preserve the root ball and finally safely remove the hydrangea for replanting.

Like this plant, there is a moving day coming for the church - and I am not talking about church buildings. When Jesus comes to take his church, He is not removing facilities. He is coming for his bride - those who have received Him as Lord and Savior.

I Thessalonians 4:17 encourages us to always be ready to moving day.

"For the Lord, himself will descend from heaven with a shout, with the voice of an archangel, and the trumpet of God. And the dead in Christ will rise first. Then we who are alive and remain shall be caught up together with them."

The Greek for "caught up" is *harpazo* that literally means to be taken away by force. Just like the force I used to relocate my little plant, God will use the force necessary to relocate us to be with Him.

Sometimes we will feel that force relocating us to a more fruitful place here on the earth. Such moves might seem like a dirty and difficult business. These moves are seldom easy. Saying good-bye to friends and family is never fun. Job changes usually include a part of us that will need change to meet the required needs of the new employment. And woe be to the parent who must enforce the changes required by the new school.

Yes, change is difficult, and moving is quite a challenge. But, the result is well worth the effort spent. I am so glad that our final move will only require the relationship with the Savior who has paid every cost to bring us to our eternal destination.

Today as that wonderful day draws near.
May we all keep that listening ear,
to respond to the heavenly trumpets call
and leave this earth once and for all.

Seldom Early and Never Late

Did you ever have one of those days, or maybe even weeks, when you were assailed on every side? It seems that we all do have times that leave us winded, worn, weary, and weak. Those times tend to drain us of our physical, spiritual, and emotional energy.

It is in just such a time like these that we can go to Psalm 20. This Bible passage puts the "E" in encouragement and the focus right back on the Father who allows the events but never lets us be overwhelmed by the circumstances. Take a long look at this passage to help you in your time of need.

May the LORD answer you in the day of trouble -----*Help!*
May the name of the God of Jacob defend
you---------*Jesus!*
May He send you help from the sanctuary---------------*Back
to the temple!*
And strengthen you out of Zion----------------------------
Need that!
May He remember your offerings-------------*Though they
were given freely.*
And accept your burnt sacrifice---------------*The death of
the old nature.*
Selah -------------------------------------- *Now stop and
think about that.*

May He grant you according to your heart's
desire-------*Him!*
And fulfill all your purpose------------------*His will for our
lives.*
We will rejoice in your salvation-------------*A personal
choice to praise Him.*
And in the name of our God we will set up banners---------
We will tell the world.
May The LORD fulfill all your petitions-----------------
Answers your prayers.
Now I know that the LORD saves His anointed-------*When
did He ever let you down?*
He will answer him from His holy heaven------------*God
hears our every prayer from heaven.*
With saving strength of His right hand-----------*When your
strength is gone He has a reserve.*
Some trust in chariots-----------------------------*He says
trust in Me!*
Some in horses------------------------*He wants to be our
strength!*
But we will remember the name of the LORD our God---
There is power in the name!
They have bowed down and fallen-------------*The fate of
our enemies!*
But, we have risen and stand upright-----------*God will
stand you back up on your feet.*
**Save LORD! ----------*My favorite words because I use
them so often!***
May the King answer us when we call ------*make sure you
have Him on speed dial!*

There have been times in my mind,
That I thought that God's pace lagged behind,
Only later with hind sight to see,
That His timing turned out best for me.

In these trials that teach us how to wait,
God is seldom early and never late!

All Systems Go

Wow, it is sometimes such a hard thing to face the daily news. As I read about an earthquake in China, the trouble in ancient Burma, and the persistent issues of the Middle East, I realize that I can be easily overwhelmed with current events.

When we see so much suffering and cruelty, it can be no surprise that we often wonder,

"How much farther downward can this world go?"

Chapters 7 and 8 in 2 Thessalonians can provide us an answer to that question:

"For the mystery of lawlessness is already at work; only He who now restrains will do so until He is taken out of the way. And then the lawless one will be revealed . . . ."

I am sure I don't have to tell you lawlessness is at work both at home and abroad. This lawlessness runs from traffic violations (which can really be frustrating), to the current war in the Middle East.

It is more than a comfort to know that God is restraining the complete moral breakdown of our world until He is ready to remove His Holy Spirit and then reveal the *lawless one (the antichrist).*

Before you have a second to be concerned about that situation, allow me to remind you that when God removes His Holy Spirit we will be taken out! That will bring a green light that will usher us into His presence. Now instead of dreading the daily news we can find ourselves encouraged as we see all things getting ready for that great day.

Luke 21:36 says, "Pray always that you may be counted worthy to escape all these things that will come to pass and stand before the Son of Man."

So, tomorrow when more bad news is about to appear on the front page, just read it, pray, and remember that someone else is about to appear on the center stage. It will not be too long. Can you hear it? It sounds like the NASA launch site rumbling in the distance, "attention, attention, all systems are now ---- Go, Go, Go!"

What You Can Do

Even blessings can sometimes be a challenge. Take, for instance, the blessing of ministry. Yes, we prayed for a ministry, and felt honored by a heavenly call. Yet, when facing the enormity of the task we just might not feel up to the challenge.

Here is a little poem to help you walk through the door that God is now opening in your life. It is my prayer for you that you find in it the encouragement to answer your "call".

Just Me

What God can you do with me?
I feel so lost with the task I see.
I need more of You and less me.
Oh, God what you can you do with me?

Where is the strength to heed your call?
I know you are great,
But Lord, I'm small.
And there are others, who seem so much more equipped
    I see,
Oh, God what can you do with me?

My failings now flood my heart, my mind,
Often ashamed and often blind,
How can I do this work, this time?
Oh, God what can you do with me?

But Lord, I'll put my hope in you.
Your strength alone will see me through.
I know we've got a job to do.
Oh, God what can you do in me?

I'll commit to choose to obey.
And to follow you in all you say.
I'm sick of going my own way!
Oh, God what can you do in me?

I'm pressing on to the task,
Your lovely presence is all I ask.
And wait on you, and wait to see,
What only you can do in me.

Psalm 22:4- 5 says, "Our fathers trusted in You: They trusted, and You delivered them. They cried to You, and were delivered; they trusted in You and were not ashamed."

So, don't worry. God can do it.

Maynard G. Krebs

In 1959, there was a television show called, "The Many Lives of Dobie Gillis." I rarely missed a single episode. For those too young to remember Dobie and his friend Maynard, here are a few facts I recall from that show.

Maynard G. Krebs hated work. You see Maynard was what in those days was called, a "beatnik." In fact, one of his frequent lines was to state, very emphatically, "Work?" He used this line whenever anyone even remotely suggested that he earn a living. Maynard G. Krebs hated work!

Dobie, on the other hand, worked very hard for his father who owned a corner grocery store. These were the days before "Super Markets" and Mom and Pop stores were very common. Dobie's Dad couldn't stand Maynard. As a beatnik, Maynard was unshaven, often dirty, and began his sentences with the word "like". We can thank the 1960's for that new piece of slang. One final fact about Maynard was that he thought he was on a quest for a life more meaningful than work and responsibility.

Unfortunately, Maynard is not gone. There are a good many people just like Maynard hanging around today. Even more sad, is that these people often find themselves in the body of Christ.

When you meet them, as certainly you will, they will tell you their tale of woes and expect you to keep them in their comfortable life of "not working." This is what Maynard often did to Dobie. Oh, and let me add that he got Dobie in lots of trouble.

What does the Bible say about work and the people who choose not to work? Shouldn't we feel sorry for them? Shouldn't we help pay their bills? After all we are supposed to love our brothers - right?

Well, let's see what God's word says. In 2 Thessalonians 3:10-12, the apostle Paul wrote, "For while we were yet with you, we gave you this rule and charge: **If a man will not work, neither let him eat.** Indeed, we hear that some among you are disorderly (passing their lives in idleness, neglectful of duty), being busy with other people's affairs instead of their own work. Now we charge and exhort such persons in the Lord Jesus Christ that they work in quietness and earn their food and other necessities."

There are some very strong words in these verses. Words like "charge", "rule," and even stronger, the word "exhort." No walking on egg shells or tiptoeing around a subject for Paul. God says what He means, and God means what He says. Now you know what to say the next time you meet Maynard G. Krebs seeking your charitable heart.

The Art of Sewing

What little I have learned about sewing was not because I had a desire to sew. Rather, it has been the constraints of a tight budget and my unwillingness to pay the high cost of draperies, that made me *willing* to learn to sew.

In sewing, there are some fundamental rules to follow. If you skip steps and try to cut corners (no pun intended) you will end up with a mess every time. There are also patterns to follow. You must take special care and follow every instruction to the utmost to end up with the desired outcome.

When someone gets really good at sewing, they can create their own patterns for other people to buy (more money issues) and follow. These people work very hard to perfect their patterns looking to find every conceivable flaw before they can market their product.

The Book of Timothy is just such a pattern. It is the pattern for church leaders and the "how to guide" for training young pastors.

I Timothy 1:16 says, "However, for this reason I obtained mercy, that in me first Jesus Christ might show all long-suffering, as a *pattern* to those who are going to believe on Him for everlasting life."

Our lives in Christ first begin by receiving Christ. Then we learn how to live this new life in Christ. This is what the apostle Paul calls 'Walking in the Spirit". We get a chance to learn the pattern from those who have learned and lived it before us – the pattern to deny self and follow Jesus.

In the arena of sewing, pattern makers do not look down on pattern buyers. Pattern buyers often comment, however, that the pattern is too hard, with statements like: "I don't get it", or "what in the world was someone thinking when they made this pattern"? As time goes on, with a little patience and some good old fashioned hard work, a seamstress is born and these old patterns become "the easy game of sewing".

Today you may be trying to follow the pattern of other Christians who have gone before you. I believe in Christ there will always be someone in that position in our lives. Eventually you will become a **pattern** maker yourself leading someone else in their walk with Christ. The price for this mentoring is called "long-suffering," and the outcome far outweighs your sacrifice. In the end you will be blessed with the desired outcome – cut from the pattern to look like Jesus!

Happy Sewing!

Return to Sender

If you have ever had a letter or package that you mailed out returned to you, then you know the frustration of seeing the red stamp "return to sender". The last time this happened to me the post office included a list of various reasons why the package was returned undeliverable to me. The possible reasons included: no longer at this address, incomplete address, and addressee unknown.

Like my returned package, have you ever wondered if your prayers ever end up in an undeliverable category? If so, let's examine some of the most likely reasons.

1. No longer at this address: Thankfully this not a problem. God is omnipresent. Omnipresent is just a way of saying that God can be everywhere at once.

2. Incomplete Address: I think there are a number of people who get stuck here. For instance, many people believe in God as a cosmic force of the universe and not a personal God of the Bible. Throwing up a "flare prayer" to just any old cosmic force has no valid address.

3. Addressee Unknown: You wouldn't think this could be a problem, but there are many people who address their prayers to saints, angels, and other unknown deities. If

you expect the God of the Bible to hear and answer your prayers, you might want to make sure you know Him first.

I Timothy 2:5 gives us clear delivery instructions for our prayers.

"For there is One God and one Mediator between God and men –the man Christ Jesus."

Mediator means a person who serves as an intermediary to reconcile differences. It is a great comfort to know that I have someone who is helping to reconcile my prayer needs and to deliver them to the heavenly Father.

It is important to take time and pray!

It is more important to do what is required so that our prayers will be delivered.

Today the message is clear – God is able and ready to hear!
When our prayers are sent through The Son,
We can be sure the message has begun,
To reach the Father's listening ear
And know an answer is very near.

These requests that time and space could never hinder,
will never see – "Return to Sender."

Kindly Step Aside

"What in the world is *this* world coming to?" I bet you have said words just like that at one time or another. Yesterday, I was walking around our outdoor mall and was nearly run down by both people and cars. In a trip to the ice cream shop, my husband was nearly knocked to the floor by a man leaving the line. We were both a little dazed and also amazed by the rude behavior we so often see in our present culture. Have you been there?

2 Timothy 3:1-5 says, "But know this, that in the last days perilous times will come; for men will be lovers of themselves, lovers of money, boasters, proud, blasphemers, disobedient to parents, unthankful, unholy, unloving, unforgiving, slanderers, without self-control, brutal, despisers of good, traitors, headstrong, haughty, lovers of pleasure rather than lovers of God. Having a form of godliness but denying its power. And from such people turn aside."

Well, I bet I don't need to tell you how true this Bible passage happens to be. So, what response should we give when treated with rude behavior? Well for starters, we can make sure our own conduct does not reflect the very poor behavior we oppose.

But, are you intrigued by the fifth verse? ("Having a form of godliness but denying its power.")

Here is the prescription for the problem of rude, rotten behavior. It can only be through the employment of the power of God that any of us can ever possess lasting change.

This part of the verse identifies the root cause of all uncivil, unprofessional, and just downright rude behavior. These people most likely believe in behaving better, but unless they are seeking after God and asking Him to change their hearts, their behavior does not reflect their beliefs. You cannot live a consistent Godly life without the power of the Holy Spirit active in your life. Your flesh will never be your friend. It will always compel you to "look out for number one" and not for the interests of others. The final part of the verse tells you what to do when faced with difficult people and their bad behavior, "*__And from such people turn away!__*"

Let the Holy Spirit be your strength! He alone can give you the power to turn away and forgo the desire to retaliate when we are treated poorly.

Today allow the Holy Spirit change your heart and be your guide

He will give you the ability and wisdom to **kindly step aside.**

The Next Step

Learning any new dance is a tricky business. Your feet usually do not want to cooperate at first. They want to do what they have always done. It takes time to discipline your feet and to learn the new steps to understand the dance. This is exactly how our lives are when we come to Christ. We have to learn a few new dance steps.

Acts 2:38 tells us, "Repent, and let every one of you be baptized in the name of Jesus Christ for the remission of sins; and you shall receive the gift of the Holy Spirit."

Repentance is the key. Repentance comes from a Greek word that literally means to change your mind. You can have no change of behavior, moving from a state of sin to a state of obedience without first having a change of mind. Confessing to others is the second step in the life of a new believer. Confessing to others publicly that we have repented helps us established the foundation for the other "new steps" we are going to learn. "For with the heart, one believes unto righteousness, and with the mouth confessions is made to salvation."(Romans 10:10).

Baptism is the third step in our "dancing" transformation. It is the public, outward sign of the inward truth that we have come to Christ. Baptism is our commitment to deny self and follow Jesus. We are dying to our old nature so that we may live for Him. Baptism is one of the earliest acts of obedience in the life of a Christian.

Finally, when you receive the Holy Spirit as the believers in Ephesus did (Acts 19), you will put a real kick into your spiritual dance routine. "John answered, saying to all, I indeed baptize you with water; but one mightier than I is coming, whose sandal strap I am not worthy to lose. He will baptize you with the Holy Spirit and fire" (Luke 3:16).

Jesus taught us all of these steps as He demonstrated them for us by living them out before us.

"Then Jesus came to Galilee to John at the Jordan to be baptized by him. And John tried to prevent Him, saying, "I need to be baptized by You, But Jesus answered and said to him, "Permit it to be so now, for thus it is fitting for us to fulfill all righteousness.

"When He had been baptized, Jesus came up immediately from the water; and behold, the heavens were opened to Him, and He saw the Spirit of God descending like a dove and alighting upon Him. And suddenly a voice came from heaven, saying, "This is My beloved Son, in Who I am well pleased" (Matthew 3:13-17).

Today is the day for the new dance, but before you hit the dance floor you must get your steps in order. It was only after Jesus fulfilled the previous passage that He began His earthly ministry. As you step out to obey you will eventually step up to the joy of ministry and enjoy the dance of your life.

Limbo Rock

D o you remember the Limbo Rock? If you didn't do the Limbo as a child, then perhaps you have seen it at wedding receptions. It is a funny dance with a Limbo Stick. You maneuver under the stick without touching it. Each time you pass under the stick, it gets lowered for another round. Finally it gets so low that one brave soul seems to be so limber that they are the only one left to make it under the stick. Then everyone shouts, "Limbo!" Okay, you get the point. How low can you go?

I Timothy 4:10 says, "For to this end we both labor and suffer reproach, because we trust in the living God, who is the Savior of *all* men" (emphasis added).

Sometimes a person may feel they have fallen too low. They have such a weight of guilt for their sins that they feel certain they can no longer be saved. Maybe we have also thought, "Well he/she has really gone too far this time, no hope for that one!"

Not True! For the soul who desires to repent there is not one change of being *Limbode Out* with God. No getting kicked out of the dance. No disqualification. Jesus Christ is the Savior of **all** humanity. The relief of guilt when He washes you in His own blood goes beyond any words I can share.

Unlike the Limbo the question is not "how low can you go?" The question today is, "Do you want to repent and receive Christ? His blood is sufficient to reach you if you are willing to reach up to Him, and then all heaven will shout, "Welcome."

John 1:12 says this:

"But, as many as received Him, to them He gave the right to become children of God…"

100% Pure

Many years ago the advertisement for Ivory Soap was, "100% Pure." The ad often showed a beautiful baby and said that their soap was so pure it would be the perfect to use for your baby. It must have been a good ad as so many different products today sell themselves with the "100% pure ingredients" tag on the label. Now the disclaimer is nearly 100% pure since it is impossible to ensure that there is nothing else in the mixture. So, with purity in mind, what percentage of your life can you advertise as living pure for Jesus? Do you need a disclaimer that your life is almost pure?

I Timothy 5:22 says, ". . . keep yourself pure . . . ." Pure means not mixed and free from impurities or contaminates. Interesting definition but not mixed with what? Only you can answer that question. If purity can determine the quality of a product, even to sell soap, then how much more important is purity in relation to the Christian walk?

Not very long ago there was an outbreak of salmonella in America. Many people became ill and some died. The Center for Disease Control worked endlessly seeking the source of this infection while it continued to spread. Finally the contaminate was found to be in peanut butter.

Once the source was found then the Company and plant where the products were manufactured were quickly located. Soon the word went out to the waiting public to stay away from peanut butter until all the infected products were recalled.

Purity is terrific in products that we use. Purity is even of greater importance in the person who lives for the Lord. People are blessed by a life that is lived free of the consequences of impurities. The world is blessed by the example of what it means to be and live as an authentic Christian. In Christian lingo we call this being "a witness."

Today is a good day to clean up our lives and our witness. Let the Lord clean you up again and get back to the purity of living 100% for Christ.

Women & Welfare

When I was in college, I worked three jobs and even then I almost did not make ends meet. God was always faithful and provided all my needs during a very lean financial time in my life. One day I was in a local grocery store buying a few items. I had counted my change to be sure I would have enough money to pay the cashier. As I was taking count of my change, I noticed the shopper in front of me buying steaks, and other very expensive foods. Wow, I thought, "it must be nice." Then to my surprise, the woman pulled out a handful of food stamps to pay for her items.

This event could have been a time for me to develop an attitude of resentment and bitterness. I knew that bitterness was sin, and I was not going let the devil get an advantage in this moment.

Instead, this event prompted me to wonder what God had to say about the subject of welfare. Did He have any particular plan for the church in this matter? How would His program actually work?

I Timothy 5:4 has plenty to say about provisions and in particular provisions for women in the church. "But if a widow has children or grandchildren, see to it that these are first made to understand that it is their religious duty at home, and make return to their parents or grandparents for their care, for this is acceptable in the sight of God."

So, the provision for widows is primarily the responsibility of their family. What if there is not a family? Well the Bible has taken care of that situation too. "Let no one be put on the roll of widows (who receive church support) who is under sixty years old or who has been the wife of more than one man, she must have a reputation for good works, as one who has brought up children, who practiced hospitality to strangers, washed the feet of the disciples, helped to relieve the distressed, and devoted herself to diligently doing good in every way" (Tim. 5: 9-10).

Yes, there is church support for those over 60 who are in the business of serving the body and living exemplary lives. What about younger women, and don't forget about the food stamps - where are they in the Bible?

1 Tim 5:11 says, "Refuse younger widows, for they will become restive and when their natural desires grow strong, they will withdraw against Christ and wish to marry again." The idea is that they will want to marry and should do so. The word withdraw means that they would withdraw from serving Christ only.

The "food stamps" in the Bible were opportunities for those in need to follow reapers and pick up the left over grain of harvested fields to meet their needs. (See The Book of Ruth.) This practice is still current. I have learned that in some areas the poor are allowed to pick the remaining produce once the pickers have completed their harvest.

So, what about welfare? Well, for those not financially faring well there are a few things a woman can do. First seek God, Second seek work, Third seek assistance and counsel from the church, Fourth consider marrying and lastly look for ways to be productive even if it requires picking produce.

Human Resources Department

No matter where you work, there is probably some sort of department that manages human resources. The people who work in this department handle your hiring process and unfortunately, the not so happy firing process.

My first job out of college, I was as a business manager for The Culligan Water Conditioning Company. It was not a large enough franchise to have an official HR department. So, the HR responsibilities were added to my job description as "other duties as assigned."

I was blessed to have a wonderful Christian boss who also was the owner the franchise. He had a very kind heart and always tried to give people in the church a job. Unfortunately, some of these new Christians (and even on occasion, an older Christian) didn't really work out. It seems that the reason these people needed work was that they really did not want to work. Once their poor work ethic became evident, I had the not so joyous part of my job – recommending to my boss that the individual be fired.

One day my boss came into my office and said, "We are not going to hire anymore Christians!" I was shocked. Seeing my expression he went on to explain that these folks, more often than not, thought that because he was a Christians they didn't have to "really" work when he hired them.

It is interesting to me that the apostle Paul went through the same issue. Maybe it shouldn't surprise me. Even though a great deal of time has passed between Paul and my Culligan boss, the nature of the human heart has not changed over time. Fortunately, Paul has left us instruction on the work ethic in the Bible and how that work ethic is supposed to play out in the life of a believer.

I Timothy 6:1 says, "Let as many bondservants as are under the yoke count their own masters (employers) worthy of all honor, so that the name of God and His doctrine may not be blasphemed. And those who have believing masters (employers), let them not despise them because they are brethren (Christians), but rather serve (labor) for them because those who are benefited are believers and beloved. Teach and exhort these things."

So, Christians ought to be the best employees in business and their work ethic should serve as a great witness for Christ. Fortunately, my former boss did finally find some Christians who had learned this Biblical principle and they did become a blessing to our office. Not to mention it sure made my job a lot easier as the lone member of the HR department.

The Tango

Did you ever hear the old saying that, "it takes two to Tango?" Most likely a large number of you heard these words during your growing up years. I know that I sure did. It usually takes some personal experience in life to prove these old adages true. I don't know if the apostle Paul ever heard it said this way but he seems to have understood the concept.

I Timothy 6:3-5 says, "If anyone teaches otherwise and does not consent to wholesome words, even the words of our Lord Jesus Christ, and to the doctrine which accords with godliness, he is proud, knowing nothing, but is obsessed with disputes and arguments over words, from which come envy, strife, reviling, evil suspicions, useless wrangling of men of corrupt minds and destitute of the truth, who suppose that godliness is a means of gain. From such withdraw yourself."

Some people ask sincere questions when they want to learn. For these folks, I am ready, willing and with God's help, able to answer their questions. There are other people who just want to wear you out with disputes, debates, and wrangling over anything and everything that comes up. These people are really not seeking to discover the truth.

All they want to do is verbally tussle and word wrestle. In a word, all they really want to do is Tango, but dancing the Tango requires a great deal of physical and emotional energy. Doing this dance can leave you weary, worn and just to drained to serve those who are genuinely seeking God and who might need your assistance.

When I was a child I was warned about Bullies. It seems they didn't all go away when I grew up. These are the people who are always looking for a fight. They will take you on if you are foolish enough to jump on the dance floor with them. They have learned that they cannot engage in physical aspects of the bully so they try to fight with words in new and creative ways, like debating, disputing, and arguing.

Paul has some compelling advice for those of us who end up facing "the verbal bully." Just stay away from a person like that – withdraw yourself. Yes, just walk away and stay away. It is not about your ability to argue your case. It is not about matching their intellect and driving home the correct answer - even when you know for sure that you are in the right. It will always take a person of strong character to walk away. So, walk away and remember - we don't have time to Tango today!

My God, My God

Oh, I bet you know the rest of this verse, "My God, My God, why have you forsaken me?

Why are You so far from helping me and from the words of my groaning?" (Psalm 22: 1)

Psalm 22 is referred to as a Messianic psalm meaning it has a direct application to the coming Messiah. The very words spoken by Jesus from the cross were contained in a Psalm written well before Jesus spoke them. The pain of His lament was not only physical in its anguish but emotional and spiritual as well. Until the moment of the cross, Jesus had never been separated from the Father. When our sin was placed upon Him at Calvary, the Father was compelled to look away, to separate Himself from the Son.

Today a commonly used phrase is "Oh my god." It can be an expletive spoken for everything from a broken finger nail to the death of a loved one. While I think it a bad use of language, it may often express a deep cry for help, of regret, or a deep loss of one sort or another.

The problem is that the "my" part of that phrase is not well thought out. Oh, when I find myself in deep water I do cry to "MY" God. My question, to those who use the phrase, is "who is your god?" When I am confident of His presence with me I can do anything. Separated from Him, I find I can't do anything at all.

If today you find yourself crying out to God, ask yourself if you are feeling separated from Him. Jesus took all our sin to Calvary but the effect of God's grace is only as good as your willingness to call out to Him. Think of what you know to be true of God and reconcile yourself to Him. Here is a little rhyme to help you get started.

Other gods have failed me,
And left me in distress.
Oh, Jesus please rescue me
From another earthly mess!

What Are You Crowing About

Today, while on my morning walk, I came upon a big, black crow. When we were only feet apart he began to really tell me off with his "crowing." Of course I have no idea what in the world he was having such a fit about, but he sure was making a lot of noise.

I think many people are like that bird. There are many people making a lot of noise, a lot of crowing, but no real substance within their speech. I think of "the big issues" like, "Y-2K" that had the media and the entire world in frenzy, the economy on the brink of collapse, and you know the result - "Y-2K" never happened!

I am old enough to remember the Cuban Missile Crisis. I had a neighbor who built a bomb shelter in their yard. And you know what? They never had the occasion to use it. The noisy "big issues" get big headlines and then fizzle into nothingness. If we are going to make some noise, then let's expend the energy about the certainty of eternity.

2 Timothy 1:8 says "Do not be ashamed to testify to and for our Lord, nor of me, a prisoner for His sake, but take your share of the suffering of the Gospel in the power of God. For it is He who delivered and saved us and called us with a calling itself holy and leading to holiness not because of anything of merit that we have done, but because of and

to further His own purpose and grace which was given us in Christ Jesus before the world began."

In short, go tell the world about Jesus! Yes, you will suffer at the hands of those who don't want to hear it, but God has saved you! Remember, someone took the risk to tell you about Jesus. Go tell the world about Jesus! That is what God has called us to do. His plan is to use you and me to tell the whole world about His only begotten Son. Now, that's something to crow about!

Golden Retriever or Poodle

I just love dogs. I have loved them all my life. I have owned a dog nearly my entire life. They are super companions. In fact, I just can't seem to pass by a puppy without asking the owner if I can hold it.

One of my favorite breeds is the Golden Retriever. Though they are big, hairy and seem to have endless energy they are wonderfully loyal. They will do your bidding without any hesitation. Even when they have retrieved over and over and over again, they cannot help but go for that ball one more time. Then they will come lay at your feet and look up at you with total contentment. That's my kind of dog!

On the other hand my, Aunt has a couple of little Poodles. These dogs are finicky and fickle. When they want to love you — they do so on their own terms. When they don't want to love you well, they don't. Life is their way or the highway. No kidding. When these dogs are left alone they will get even with you for leaving them. They find some rotten way to make you miserable. Thank God I don't own a Poodle!

The apostle Paul, when writing his last letter, had similar experiences with people.

In 2 Timothy 1:13-17, Paul makes the following statement, "Hold fast the pattern of sound words which you have heard from me, in faith and love which are in Christ Jesus. That good thing which was committed to you, keep by the

Holy Spirit who dwells in us. This you know that all those in Asia have turned away from me, among whom are Phygellus and Hermongenes. The Lord grant mercy to the household of Onesiphorus, for he often refreshed me, and was not ashamed of my chains; but, when he arrived in Rome, he sought me out very zealously and found me."

Do you see a Poodle here? How about a Retriever? Paul had the Word of God to offer at the end of his life, but he didn't have much of anything else. When the chips were down and he was about to give his life for Christ, the folks in Asia turned away. His imprisonment was a little too low for their taste. The price of the Gospel got a little too tough. Those who were not able to maintain their faith deserted Paul. Thank God for Onesiphorus! He was loyal. He was not turned off by Paul's chains. You could even say he was a retriever. Yes, willing and zealously seeking his teacher in the faith - even when it wasn't fun.

Our white Lab will run for that ball no matter how many times you throw it. He will willingly, zealously give himself until he falls at your feet. There is nothing that will dazzle him or draw him from his task. He only seeks to please his master and obey when asked.

I believe God made the Retriever this way to show us what loyalty looks like. So, the next time that you hear your master call remember it is the joy of obedience and not the ball that draws you to respond and run to God and learn a lesson from a dog.

A Little Sleep, A Little Slumber

"A little sleep, a little slumber, a little folding of the hands to lie down and sleep. So will your poverty come like a robber and your want like an armed man" (Proverbs 6: 10- 11).

Coming to know Christ and then being forgiven from the burden of your sins is an amazing and wonderful thing. The day you stand up for Christ and tell others what He has done for you, will bless your socks off - but then what?

Well for starters, many people simply go back to their same old daily grind. They eat, work, and sleep through all the other concerns of this life. Before you know it, the joy of your salvation has become something that happened in your past. The future is found in chasing the old goals: pleasure, possession, power, and prestige. As for the Christian experience, well it was good while the emotions lasted. Then we can drift away neglecting Bible reading, Bible study, and even find excuses for not going to church, in short we fall asleep at the wheel.

Then suddenly you discover that your life is in the hopper again. Things don't work out with the power gig. The money runs out, and the relationships don't pan out. What happened? Quite simply, your "want" or needs did not fulfill and suddenly you are back to your knees and back to the

139

throne room of the Father. "A little sleep, a little slumber a little folding of the hands perhaps?

To diagnose the root cause of this drifting, we need to take a trip back to the day of our salvation. Back to the love and grateful heart we had for God the moment He forgave us and gave us a future with Him. The result of those days can be expressed in one word – joy!

Then the appetites of the "old life" arise and begin to call us back to the things that never gave us joy. Yes, it is so easy to go to sleep at the wheel.

We are in an active warfare! A sentry asleep at the post puts everyone in danger, even if that sentry is you. Fortunately, we are in good company. Remember in Luke 9:32 where the disciples fell asleep in the Garden of Gethsemane. Jesus told them to wake up, get busy, and pray. The best part of that story is when they awoke; they saw the glory of Jesus.

Today - "Awake, O sleeper, and arise from the dead, and Christ shall shine upon you and give you light. Look carefully then how you walk! Live purposefully and worthily and accurately, not as the unwise and witless, but as wise, making the most of your time, because the days are evil" (Ephesians 5:14-16). Do you hear the alarm going off? It's time to come out of sleep mode.

Weedy Business

Working in the garden always puts me in a good place to learn from God and His creation.

While pulling weeds today I was astonished! Those bad guys in my garden seldom grow out in the open for all to see and me to weed. They grow right under the foliage of my tender plants! They even entangle their weedy roots in with the roots of my flowers. In worst cases, I even have to remove my plants, clean the roots off, and then transplant them to get them to grow in a healthy manner.

Well, there are weeds in the garden of God, namely corrupt men and women within the church.

Like a master gardener, the Lord has given us direction on just how to handle these spiritual weeds too. In 1 Timothy 3:1-9 the apostle Paul writes:

"But know this, that in the last days, perilous times will come. For men will be lovers of themselves, lovers of money, boasters, proud, blasphemers, disobedient to parents, unthankful, unholy, unloving, unforgiving, slanderers, without self-control, brutal, despisers of good, traitors, headstrong, haughty, lovers of pleasure rather than lovers of God, having a form of godliness but denying it's power. And from such people turn away! For this sort are those who creep into households and make captive of gullible women loaded down with sins, led away by various lusts, always learning and never able to come to the knowledge of the truth. Now as Jannes and Jambres resisted Moses, so do these also resist the truth: concerning faith, but they will progress no further, for their folly will be manifest to all, as theirs also was."

You know I never worry about the weeds I cannot see. I remove the ones I can see and then I know that before long, the hidden, ugly weed will grow and become visible for me to pull out also. This is how it is for those who guide, and care for the body of Christ - the church. You let God reveal the weeding for today and pull the bigger weeds when they show themselves for what they are. Tending to the body of Christ is like caring for the garden. All kidding aside, its weedy business!

Something Stinks

After being gone on a trip for a few days, I was so happy to get back home.

It is nice to get away for awhile but always better to come home. I unlocked the door in happy anticipation but was greeted by this terrible, rotten odor. What was that smell?

Apparently before our departure, we forgot to run the garbage disposal and now the whole house reeked with this foul odor. All we could do was hold our breath, open some windows, light some scented candles, and clean out the disposal.

That rotten smell reminded me of what it must be like for a worldly person when they come in contact with an authentic Christian. Did you ever stop to consider that we have a rotten smell to those around us who have not yet committed their lives to Jesus? We smell rotten to them. A Christian who is dying to the flesh brings that odor of death to those who are not walking in Christ. It is the stench of death to their flesh, and they will do to you exactly what I did to that mess in my disposal – do their best to get rid of it as quickly as possible.

Rejection hurts. I believe the emotional pain of rejection hurts more than any physical malady. It leaves you questioning yourself and wondering, "What's wrong with me?" The truth is there is nothing wrong with you. The problem is your life in Christ is light shining in the darkness of sin and that light is like the stench of rotting flesh. No one wants to be around the smell of death.

2 Timothy 3:12 says "Yes, **all** who desire to live godly in Christ Jesus **will** suffer persecution." Did you realize that rejection is persecution? How many Christian are going to have this unhappy experience of rejection? We all are going to experience some level of rejection and some level of persecution for our faith. It can be as subtle as being passed over for promotion at work or literally being killed for our faith and in Christ. Consequently, we should examine ourselves and make sure we do not fall prey to compromise for the sake of acceptance.

After all, not everyone wants your life to expose their sin.

2 Cr. 2:15 & 16 says these encouraging words;

"For we are to God the fragrance of Christ among those who are being saved and among those who are perishing. To the one we are the aroma of death leading to death, and to the other the aroma of life leading to life."

Having to endure rejection is part of the cost of walking with Jesus. He said if we deny Him before men He will deny us before the Father. I would rather receive the sting of rejection from the world than be without Jesus. Remember the world is not rejecting you – it is Jesus they think really stinks.

Nein

Having children is such a wonderful experience. I think God made these little ones so darling because He knew that raising them would not always be fun.

On one of our military assignments, we were living in Frederick, Maryland. My husband was working with the United States Army Medical Research and Development Command. A German scientist and his family were assigned to our military post on a scientific exchange program. We had the opportunity to be their host family. They were such a delight, and it was also a learning experience for our entire family.

Marcus and Uta had three darling children, but it was little Hannah who won my heart. She looked exactly like the Campbell Soup girl. She had beautiful blond hair, big blue eyes, and the rosiest cheeks I had ever seen. She was like a little china doll. Since she was so easy to love, I indulged her with lots of attention and cookies. There was no doubt about it, Hannah and I had a special connection.

One day, near the end of their assignment, her parents came by our home to drop something off. Hannah quickly got out of the car and ran to the door. Her parents very busy with the upcoming move had no intention of coming inside. They had lots of errands to run with no time to spare. Hannah, on the other hand, had every intention of coming inside. She knew the treats and attention on the other side of that door, and she was surely coming in to get them.

Her parents had already said good bye and were heading for the car. Noticing that little Hannah had not followed them called out in firm German, "Hannah, kommen hier jetzt bitte." I understood them to tell Hannah, "come here now, please." Hannah said softly in reply, "nein." Her father, a true force to be reckoned with, repeated himself, but in command style, "Hannah, kommen hier jetzt bitte." Again, Hannah replied with a very calm but resolute, "nein." Nearing a nuclear meltdown, her father, a full 6' 6", rose up and commanded once more, "Hannah! Come!" This time little Hannah rose up to her own height, which was something for her own little three years of age. She put her hands on her hips, then raising her heel to her buttocks she kicked that foot three times and shouted, "Nein, nein, nein." Well, I bet I don't have to tell you who won that battle, and Hannah was the sorry one for having begun the fight.

Many times we are all like that determined little child. We reach for something we should leave alone. We plan to do something we should not be doing, and then we hear the voice of the Father saying "come." Oh, but we so want what we want! We may answer at first in a somewhat reverent way, "no." The Father, knowing what we can never know, does what is best for us again by saying "come." Now in the voice of our flesh we answer yet again, "No!" The Father loves us so much that now He is forced to bring the painful consequences for our little acts of rebellion and temper tantrums. Can you see our little feet kicking as we scream, "Why is the happening to me?"

In the end, God will win the battle, after all He is God. We are the ones (like Hannah) who are so sorry we started the fight. The entire struggle could have been averted by knowing God's Word. All this could also have been stopped by our believing that Father really does know best.

Psalm 23 begins with these words, "The Lord is my shepherd; I shall not want."

When we understand that we are in the hands of a loving shepherd we will also know that "WANT" can truly be our enemy and cause us all manner discomfort. Today is the perfect day to say "I will obey", and understand that The Father does know what is best.

Finally, let's all say good bye to the little word I learned from Hannah, "Nein."

Bugged

Is life bugging you? How about people? It should come as no surprise that we are having experiences that bug us in the world today. After all, the world is a "buggy" place. So, we expect things in the world to be an irritation but what about within the body of Christ?

Psalm 23:5 says, "You prepare a table before me in the presence of my enemies; You anoint my head with oil; My cup runs over."

These "bug" problems are not new, no matter where they appear. Shepherds had this problem with their sheep and after all we are the Lord's - right?

A shepherd had a few things with him at all times to protect the flock. One thing was a horn of oil. You see sheep sometimes fight. They butt heads. Sound familiar? The cure was to pour oil on their heads. Oil is the Biblical symbol for the Holy Spirit. What we need when we butt heads with others is the fruit of the Holy Spirit, which is love. Love has the ability to help us let things slide - just like the oil helps the sheep slide off each other when they start butting heads.

Also, sheep had problems with bugs. When a shepherd saw bugs infesting his sheep, he would pour oil over them.

The oil would suffocate the bugs and all would be well again with the sheep.

Once again with the oil of the love of God we can choose to be loving and merciful to the silly little things that bug us.

As we allow our Shepherd to anoint us with more and more of His Spirit, we find we have more and more love. Only then do we learn that the things we were fighting about and being bugged about were the workings of the enemy to cause division within the church.

The good news is that the love of God is stronger than the hate of the enemy. Today, if you will allow your Shepherd to anoint you with His love, you won't have to be bugged anymore.

Cool in the Pool

As I sit writing this devotion, there has been a heat wave blanketing our city. The grass is dry, and the flowers are limp from the daily baking of the sun. Everywhere I go, people are talking about how long these temperatures might last. I even heard some folks saying they were afraid it was going to be a very long and hot summer.

One afternoon, I headed to the pool. I had a doubt or two about whether the pool water was going to provide any relief to this stifling heat. I decided to give it a shot. It was amazing. Not only was it cool in the pool, but it was cool on the deck area near the pool. Suddenly the temperatures in the 100 degree range seemed to be no big deal. I was refreshed, relaxed, and even enjoyed this summer blast.

Life is sure like that heat wave. Some days you wonder how long your trouble is going to last. Some people may even question if it will be lifelong trouble. Yet, there is a river you can visit when the heat of life dries you out.

Psalms 46: 4-7 reads:

"There is a river whose streams shall make glad the city
    of God,
The holy place of the tabernacle of the Most High,
God is in the midst of her; she shall not be moved,

God shall help her, just at the break of dawn,
The nations raged, the kingdoms were moved;
He uttered His voice, the earth melted.
The Lord of hosts is with us.
The God of Jacob is our refuge."

Come on, get your suit on! Jump in the river and enjoy the swim. Be refreshed while you trust your heavenly Father. He can handle the heat. When you find yourself worn, weary, and wondering, go to this river, and remember it is always cool in this pool.

Have You Heard

Three books from the Old Testament: Samuel, Kings, and Chronicles are some of the most entertaining books of the Bible. These are the books of stories of real people and their relationships. Love stories, war stories, and more family issues than I have room to write about. Relationships always involve the human heart. When we deal with the heart, the sad emotions of loneliness and hopelessness are bound to come up.

In 1 Samuel, Chapter 1, Hannah (which has many meanings to include grace, and passion), had a broken heart. Treated badly by her husband's other wife and childless, Hannah had a difficult road to walk. She did the logical thing and went to her husband who really didn't understand her sorrow. She went to the priest who thought she was drunk. Finally, she went where we can always go when we are in need of understanding – to the Lord. At this point the priest conferred a blessing on her and she returned home hopeful and full of expectations for what the Lord was going to do for her.

1Samuel 1:18 says:

"And she said, 'Let you maidservant find favor in your sight.'

So, the woman went her way and ate, and her face was no longer sad."

She went home without a child. She still had her husband's other wife with whom she still had to contend with. She had a husband who loved her but still did not understand her heart. Yet, she was no longer sad. What happened to Hannah? Her greatest sorrow was being misunderstood, but God understood her heart, her desire for a child, and He would fulfill the natural desire He had placed within her.

Hannah had been to the throne of the Father and left with faith. Not faith in People, but she put her faith in the one who is always faithful. Everyone has at one time or another been misunderstood, lonely, and felt they had nowhere to go with their broken hearts. For all of us in need, Hannah is a great example to follow in those difficult times.

Go to the Father, He is a good listener. Go to the Father, He is omniscient - knowing all. When you do, make sure you leave like Hannah and return home filled with joy. God will do it!

This is what Hannah did, God heard, and Samuel was the answer to her prayer. Oh, by the way did you know that the name *Samuel* means - Heard!

Come Fly with Me

Shortly after the horrendous events of what we now call "9-11," it seemed as if the entire country was shaking in fear. Even so, I had made some travel plans and was scheduled to fly out of town on vacation. The thought of similar events happening to me on my flight had more than crossed my mind. I simply resolved that I would not be crippled by fear. Causing me to live in fear was what the terrorists hoped to accomplish. I was not about to succumb to their objective.

So, I went on my vacation, and I had a wonderful time. I will admit to a few anxious moments. I had to refocus and manage my emotions, as my husband would say. I simply told my fears to "get lost." When I returned home, I got quite a nervous call from one of my children. The conversation started something like this, "Are you completely crazy? Don't you know you were flying over the Pacific Ocean? I am so glad that you are home. Don't do this again - OK?"

I think my son wanted to tell me this before I departed but was afraid that he might cause me to panic. Isn't that interesting? He had concern for my safety but refused to tell me fearing that he might make me afraid. As a child, I too can remember being engulfed by fears. You might say I was frozen from fears and not living a full life because of them. Thank God for Jesus!

Psalms 61:2 says this:

"From the end of the earth I will cry to You.
When my heart is overwhelmed;
Lead me to the rock that is higher than I."

I am now no longer frozen in fear - my life is full. I have discovered that fear is a choice. I would rather put my trust in Jesus than succumb to my earthly fears. That is why I can invite you today to leave your fears behind you, and as the airline advertisement so aptly proclaims, "come fly with me."

Tick Tock

Do you hear the clock? The night is sometimes long, especially if you are sick or troubled.

Tick Tock - it can be miserable listening to that clock. Forcing yourself to lie down, hearing every sound. You wonder if you will ever fall asleep. No more energy to weep. Your mind can run like the wind, and then you hear that sound again - Tick Tock. Been there? Me too!

Psalm 25: 1-5 says:

"To You, O LORD, I lift up my soul,
O my God, I trust in You;
Let me not be ashamed;
Let not my enemies triumph over me.
Indeed, let no one who waits on You be ashamed;
Let those be ashamed who deal treacherously without
    cause.
Show me Your ways, O LORD;
Teach me Your paths.
Lead me in Your truth and teach me,
For You are the God of my salvation;
On You I wait all day."

In these moments, I can lift up my soul (my mind, my will, and my emotions) to the Lord. My mind keeps racing because it has run out of ways to fix my current circumstance. My will is always a problem because I want things my way — oh, don't we all. My emotions only cause me grief because I allow them to race like a runaway train.

On the other hand, I can will, I can choose, and I can decide to invest my out of control soul in God. I do ask Him to come through for me. I know others are watching. I know people hear me say that I trust Him. In fact, I want everyone who trusts Him to be blessed. Why? I want the world to know that Jesus saves, and I want those who choose evil to know that God repays.

I always know I have need of more lessons when I am hearing that clock again. God can only teach me when I bow and agree to be teachable. I know the answers are in His truth - His Word.

I also know I can only get them when I actually read it.

Once again He saves me from all my distress, but I am going to have to wait on Him for the rest.

Tick - tock only God can silence your clock. Only you can choose to allow Him to give you rest too.

Follow the Bouncing Ball

I bet you remember from childhood how to follow the bouncing ball. If you are not familiar with the phrase, "follow the bouncing ball," then let me explain. The bouncing ball was a tool to help children learn songs in cartoons. It was very popular with the television program, "The Wonderful World of Disney." It was a visual means of teaching you how to sing a new song. It really worked too!

The apostle Paul used a similar technique in his writing to his young protégé, Titus. In writing to Titus, Paul instructs us on the behavior expected for each gender and age group. He bounces from one group to the other with specific guidance for each group.

Care to try it?

Titus 2: 2:
"that the **older men be** *sober, reverent, temperate, sound in faith, in love and patience*

2:3:
"the **older women** likewise, that they be *reverent in behavior, not slanderers,*
not given to much wine, teachers of good things, that they admonish younger
Women.

younger women *to love their husbands, to love their children, to be discreet, chaste, homemakers, good, obedient to their own husbands,*

And all this so that the word of God may not be blasphemed."

2:6:

"Likewise, exhort the **young men** to be *sober minded in all things, show yourself to be a pattern of good works: in doctrine showing integrity, reverence, incorruptibility, sound speech* that cannot be condemned, that one who is an opponent may be ashamed, having nothing evil to say of you"

2:9:

"Exhort bondservants (this is present day **employees** -those who work by choice) to be *obedient to their masters, to be well pleasing in all things, not answering back, not pilfering, but showing all good fidelity, that they may adorn the doctrine of God our Savior in all things."*

So often I hear people saying they just don't know what God wants them to do. Today, if that someone is you, just follow the bouncing ball.

The Safety Patrol

When I was growing up, the elementary schools had safety patrol officers. These were actually children in our school who performed the safety function of cross walk guards for other students. They were usually chosen because they were model students and could be trusted with authority over other students.

Authority does not usually make someone popular. None of us really loves having someone tell us what we can or cannot do. Such was the case with me. I remember in third grade, walking home from school. The safety officers stood on the edge of the sidewalk. There job was to prevent students from walking into the street and to remind them to stay on the sidewalks.

One day I purposely walked around the safety officer and into the street. Frankly to this day I do not know what provoked me to do it. I simply chose to walk around the safety officer and into the street. Quickly he stood at attention and warned me that I better get out of the street and onto the sidewalk. Well, I walked right around him and into the street. He wasn't going to tell me what to do. Soon I found myself being dragged into the Principal's Office and shortly after that my father arrived at school to finish what the Principal had started. Lesson learned - don't mess with safety patrol officers.

Titus 3:1-2 shares a similar lesson:

"Remind people to be submissive to authorities, to be obedient, prepared and willing to do any upright and honorable work. To slander or abuse or speak evil of no one, to avoid being contentious and to be forbearing and to show courtesy toward everyone?"

The lesson then is the same lesson now. Obey those in authority over you. Not because the safety patrol officer or the policeman says so. No, because God says so. God has placed these people in these positions to care for us. So, we should not devise little names for them that are not complimentary either.

It is funny how things in life can turn around. When my husband and I were married, we told each other all about our lives growing up - as most couples do. It turns out that my husband was a safety patrol officer at his school and the senior officer as well. Can you imagine that?

Today, when you think of those who risk harm to keep us safe, also think of the attitude God has required of you for those who patrol for your safety.

A Trojan Horse

Most elementary school children are familiar with the Greek story of "The Trojan Horse."

Homer's epic story tells us of the strong walls of the city of Troy. The city was captured in battle with the Greeks only through the deception of "The Trojan Horse." Fooled into thinking the defeated Greeks had left a gift to their gods, the citizens of Troy unknowingly created their own disaster by bringing destruction inside their city walls. During the night, Greek warriors exited from the belly of the "horse" and ravaged the great city of Troy.

This is so like sin! When we bring something that looks good, looks fun, and looks harmless into our lives when we should be listening to the warning of the Holy Spirit, there will always be a price to pay. Our own "horses" tend to open up and pounce upon us while we rest. They turn on us with a vengeance while we slumber in spiritual sleep.

Troy only fell because they had already put their faith in false idols. They falsely believed the horse was a gift to the idols that were residing in their hearts. Maybe the Trojans were more honest then than we are now. We may say "hey, I don't have any idols," when in reality, our idols are hidden, invisible, and sometimes silent. Though they don't have visible temples, they have made their temples in our hearts and in our homes.

Specifically, these modern day idols are power, possessions, position, and pleasure.

These are the deadly Trojan horses of the modern day. Once taken inside the walls of your heart, they have the ability to destroy you.

Romans 6:12 says:

"Therefore do not let sin reign in your mortal body, that you should obey its lusts."

Galatians 5:17 says:

"For the flesh lusts against the Spirit, and the Spirit against the flesh; and these are contrary to one another, so that you do not do the things you wish."

Oh, that the Trojans had not allowed that horse through their walls of protection. Oh, that they had not given themselves over to the desires of their flesh. Oh, that we would recognize that the "Walls of Christ" will always protect us as long as we do not bring sin in.

The Word for today is victory - victory for those of you who will not permit the "horse" of sin within your walls.

Remedy for Ruin

Trouble, oh we've got trouble. I can hear the words like the sound of a train rolling down the track - trouble, trouble, trouble, trouble, trouble, trouble.

"The Music Man" is a timeless musical that was all about trouble. The con man, turned music instructor, to converted band leader is the main character. Professor Hill is what he called himself, and he made a lot more trouble than music.

Even if you have never seen the play or movie version, you probably know what it means to dance to your own beat or pipe to your own tune. We have all done it at one time or another and we have all ended up singing, "trouble, trouble, trouble."

Psalm 25 finds David singing on just such a similar tune in verses 15-18:

"My eyes are ever toward the Lord,
For He shall pluck my feet out of the net.
Turn Yourself to me, and have mercy on me,
For I am desolate and afflicted.
The troubles of my hearts have enlarged;
Bring me out of my distresses!
Look on my affliction and my pain,
And forgive my sins."

Some people, like Professor Hill, make their own trouble. Some trouble comes as a natural consequence of the sin in the Garden of Eden. It does not matter which kind of trouble you are in as, the music of desolate affliction is exactly the same - trouble, trouble, trouble.

Thankfully, there is another "Music Man" who knows exactly how to deal with these troubles. If we tune to His "music," He can pluck us out of our worst troubles because He loves us and His eyes are on us. He has already relieved us of the greatest possible trouble - the debt of our sins.

Exodus 15:2 says this;

"The Lord is my strength and song, And He has become my salvation; He is my God and I will Praise Him."

Let the train of ruin go down the track
It's trouble in plain to see,
For I am singing a heavenly song
Of my hope in Christ and His love for me.

Stranded

President Ronald Reagan was once asked, "If you were stranded on an island and could have only one book with you, what book would it be?" Without hesitation our President answered, "a Holy Bible." It seems that President Reagan realized that The Holy Bible is the only book (actually a collection of 66 books) that you can read over and over again and always find something new and relevant to your daily life – even if stranded on a deserted island.

These sorts of questions cause us to be self-reflective. What one book would I want to have if I was alone on a deserted island? Today, for fun, let's change the question. If we were stranded on an island what two things would I want to have with me?

I think Paul's personal letter to Philemon gives us a good idea of what would be most helpful. Beginning with words of encouragement, Paul writes:

"I thank my God, making mention of you always in my prayers, hearing of your love and faith which you have toward the Lord Jesus and toward all the saints, that the sharing of your faith may become effective by the acknowledgement of every good things which is in you in Christ Jesus. For we have great joy and consolation in your love, because the hearts of the saints have been refreshed by you, brother" (verses 4-7).

Like President Reagan, if I could only have one book, I too would choose The Holy Bible. God's word is still the best reading material in the world. My second choice would be a couple of saints. Our brothers and sisters in Christ are not perfect, and of course they aren't - they are just like the rest of us! Nonetheless, it is that precious fellowship with them that brings joy, love, and refreshment to our lives. We can see spiritual growth in each other and encourage each other to press on toward that finished work in Christ.

While working in my yard recently, I came upon a remnant of fall - an old leaf. No longer connected to a tree branch it was dry, cracked, and had lost all its color. That is the way it is when we do not stay in fellowship with the body of Christ. We lose our joy, our love for each other, and become dry in need of refreshment. This is what it really means is to be stranded – to be isolated and all alone.

Fortunately, we are not stranded nor alone are we? No, we can only become stranded by our own choices. This is the road to isolation - and this is how battles are won. Isolate your enemy and then go for the kill. This is Satan's battle plan for you. If he can get you isolated, then he can try to defeat you.

Do you feel like that fallen leaf, stranded, alone, dry, and cut-off? Have you chosen to break off fellowship with other believers? Are you sick of island life yet? The good ship "Body of Christ" is searching for you and I hear the captain of the ship calling -

"Welcome aboard!"

The Destroyer of Kings

Many kings have come, and many kings have gone. Their legacies are varied and interesting.

Yet, as interesting as they are and as different as their kingdoms might have been, there seems to be a common destroyer of those who become the king.

The Bible tells us plenty about the Babylonian Empire of King Nebuchadnezzar. The walled fortress of Babylon was an ancient wonder of the world. Yet, after the reign of Nebuchadnezzar, in the middle of a drunken feast, Babylon was destroyed by the Medes and Persians.

Alexander the Great was a superb military commander. Under his leadership, Greece was ruling the known world. Yet, history tells us that after a drunken night of revelry, Alexander got soaked to the bone during a rain storm, acquired pneumonia, and died. His rule of the world was a very short reign indeed.

Henry the Eighth, King of England, lived and reigned a very long while. During his reign he was known then and known now, to be a heavy drinker and a man who wouldn't keep his pants on. He died with them off, passing away in his bed with a sexually transmitted disease.

History records these stories over and over again. They all have their differences, yet they all appear to be the same. Alcohol and sexual immorality seem to destroy even the strongest of men no matter how great the strength of their kingdoms or their own personal attributes.

Scholars believe that Proverbs 31 was written by a mother. Some sources say it was the writing of Bathsheba to King Solomon. The letter is written to a prince named Lemuel, Lemuel is a name of endearment that means, belonging to God.

Can you hear this mother saying? "Now my little prince, who belongs to God, I have something to tell you."

"Do not give your strength to women, **nor your ways to that which destroys kings.** It is not for kings, O Lemuel. It is not for kings to drink wine, for princes intoxicating drink; Lest they drink and forget the law," (Proverbs 31: 3-5).

Way back then they seemed to know that the destroying duo of alcohol and sexual lust was the ruin of kings. We have historical evidence of even more kings, rulers, and presidents who have come and gone since then falling to the same ruin.

Today, mothers would do well to teach their own sons the message of this proverb. How many future leaders will live with regret about what they have done while under the influence of alcohol. Solomon was known for his wisdom. Sounds like Bathsheba knew a few things too. Proverbs 14:12 says, "There are ways that seem right to a man. But the end there of is death."

One does not need to be a king to be destroyed by the same choices that have ruined some of the greatest kings in history.

Giggle

Over last two years, I have had the joy of little visits with my grandson, Connor. Though he is just a toddler, he is able to make a big impact on the largest of adults. How does he do it? Well, without notice, every so often he just starts to giggle! It seems some of the smallest joys in life get his little giggle going. Then he gets that little giggle going on everyone else.

What makes you giggle? What small, seemingly insignificant event puts a smile on your face? Is it that one comic in the Sunday paper? Or maybe a special amusement park ride? In 1974, Ira Stanphill wrote the song "Happiness is The Lord." Here are some of the words:

Happiness is to know the Savior,
Living a life within His favor,
Having a change in my behavior,
Happiness is the Lord.

Real joy is mine,
No matter if the tear drops start.
I've found the secret,
It's Jesus in my heart!

It seems that Ira was driving his car and heard some ads for alcohol and tobacco. That ads were purporting to report on the joy and happiness those things could bring into one's life. Ira suddenly found himself singing a new little song about what really brings happiness into the life of people. It was that very event that caused him to write the above song.

Along this same line of thinking, I found a verse that brought that same joy bubbling up in me.

In Hebrews 7:25 the Bible says, "Therefore He (Jesus) is also able to save to the uttermost those who come to God through Him, since **He always lives to make intercession for them**" (emphasis added).

Knowing that Jesus loves us enough to save us is "The Good News." Knowing that Jesus has conquered sin and death, and that He is interceding on our behalf to our heavenly Father continually brings me joy. That is real love!

It is a funny thing about giggling. When you have this kind of joy it is contagious. Hearing those giggles makes others want to giggle right along with you. Ira has gone one to heaven and I bet he is giggling with the joy of knowing Jesus. How about you? Have you started to giggle yet?

Get Out of Jail Free Card

Our family loves to play board games. My husband and I probably set this habit in motion during our early courting days. Not having a lot of extra income for elaborate dates, we played board games with one another and with other couples. Our favorite game back then was *Monopoly*.

Monopoly, as many of you know, can last for many long hours. I have even known some games to go on for a day or more. This board game combines luck with strategy. For example, one aspect of luck is the space on the board called, "The Community Chest." Landing on this spot can be really good or can really set you back in the game. When you hit that spot you must pick a card. What a great feeling to choose the "get out of jail free" card. I believe there are only two of those cards in the deck. The great thing about these cards is that you can play them anytime in the game to get out of jail and continue to acquire properties.

Now *Monopoly* is a game of chance. You have to roll the dice and land on key board squares that can be critical to controlling the outcome of the game. Strategy also plays into the game. There is strategy related to making the right investments, on the right property, at the right time in the game.

While board games are fun, there is one "game" you will want to play very carefully. It is the ultimate game – the game of life. Hopefully you make good choices and wise investments. No one makes all the right choices, unfortunately. During those times of unwise choices, it would be great to be able to play a "get out of jail free" card."

This actually happened to Charles Colson. During his time with President Richard Nixon, he made some poor choices. Those choices ultimately landed him in prison. Prior to his report date to prison, he prayed to receive Jesus as Lord and Savior. He was freed from the eternal prison of life separated from God. He also was offered another "get out of jail free" card. The story goes that a Christian man close to Colson offered to serve Colson's prison sentence. Overwhelmed at this gesture from a loving Christian brother, Colson chose to serve his own sentence.

Hebrews 7:12 says:

"For I will be merciful to their unrighteousness and their sins and their lawless deeds I will remember no more."

Jesus Christ has provided the ultimate "get out of jail free" card to each of us. He served our sentence and paid the price for our lawless, sinful life choices. As if that was not enough, He completely erased the memory of those past wrongs. Just as Charles Colson has someone willing to take his punishment, Jesus is willing to take ours – but we have to choose. With Jesus Christ, you come clean, repent and use the ultimate "get out of jail free" card – the free gift of eternal life through faith in Jesus Christ.

Blackberry Pie

If you have ever lived in the South, then you know that summer is the time to pick blackberries. Picking blackberries translates into blackberry pies. Whether you serve them with vanilla ice cream or with a dollop of whipped cream, blackberry pies are the sweetest treat of summer.

While picking wild blackberries has no monetary cost, unfortunately they still come at a price. You see humans are not the only creatures who are fond of these luscious berries. It seems that little mice are drawn to those yummy berries also, and the mice draw snakes! If the snakes were not bad enough, there are also very sharp thorns and chiggers to kill your taste for these delectable berries.

Chiggers are tiny, six legged culprits that live on snakes, and other reptiles - oh yes, and humans. They bite down at the base of the hair follicle and leave you with a nasty red bump. These bumps later form a rash that can leave you itching for days. It seems that to enjoy your pie, you will have to pay the price to get it.

Adam faced this similar quandary in the Garden of Eden. The forbidden fruit looked good and he seemed to have the desire for it and the enemy also gave them the false promise of equality with God if they would just indulge in a bite. Oh, but what a price to pay for that luscious fruit - death! Adam reminds me of so many berry pickers. We seem to forget the price or believe that this time it will not come with a cost. We see the sweet fruit and remember the delicious dessert it makes and before we know it, we find ourselves suffering the consequences of our choices.

Gal 5:1 says:

"Stand fast therefore in the liberty by which Christ has made us free.
And be not again entangled with the yolk of bondage."

Believing in Jesus sets us free from sin and death. We should not return to sin and become entangled once again in that patch! It seems Satan only likes to remind us of the sweetness of sin and not the terrible bondage and cost that comes with it. Look before you leap. Ponder before you pick. Then ask yourself, are still itching for some of that pie?

A Lesson from a Master Gardener

Having spent most of our married life in the Army, we have moved all over the country and lived in many different growing zones.

When we moved to South Carolina, we entered zone eight. If you are anything like me, growing zones might not mean anything to you either. Shortly after our move to South Carolina, I was introduced to a Master Gardner. She began to teach me something new each month about zone eight. She taught me about what types of plants and flowers would grow in this region, what pests to treat for to protect my flowers, and other points of fact regarding gardens in zone eight. Soon I was teaching friends, who were also new arrivals to the southeast, and offering advice to them about their flower gardens.

One other thing my Master Gardener was very clear about – the need for weeding. I had quick fix ideas and wanted to know what spray I could use to rid myself of these nuisances. However, she explained that there really was not a quick fix for any "real" gardener. The only real cure for weeds was to spend 30 minutes per day pulling them out. It is just enough time to keep your flower beds weed free without overworking yourself. Her warning was plain, "do not allow weeds to get out of control, or they will multiply and then you really will have a big mess in front of you."

Recently, we had guests coming for a visit and the week prior I was busy preparing things for their arrival. The week they were here, I was busy enjoying spending time with them. After they left, I was busy putting the house back in order. As you probably have guessed by now, I did not spend any time weeding my garden.

Suddenly, I could hear my friend's warning about weeds. I said to myself, "Oh my goodness, I'd better take a look at my garden." Yes, as you might imagine, those rotten weeds had grown over this period of time. Some of them were bigger than my plants, and they were everywhere! How did they multiply so quickly? It had only been a few weeks. I learned a good lesson. Don't neglect the garden!

This lesson is true for the Christian walk as well. The soil of life in Christ is rich and will offer growth to almost any type of seed. We have an active enemy who is trying to grow weeds in our spiritual gardens. Being too busy for spiritual things is probably the worst spiritual weed of them all. We get too busy for prayer, too busy to read the Bible, too busy for fellowship and worship, too busy to share our faith, and too busy to build up the faith of others. There always seems to be something we would rather do than tend to our spiritual garden. Soon, the weeds that are unwanted will grow into quite a mess. Then the young gardener will be off and running to the Master Gardener for assistance and education again.

Acts 2:42 tells us how the early church lived and how we are to live in faith as well:

"And they continued steadfastly (fixed, firm, established, stable, faithful, regular and unwavering) in the apostles doctrine, and fellowship (gathering with other believers), in the breaking of bread (eating together) and prayers."

In this environment no weed can stand for long. Gardening can be fun again! While we are able to learn and grow, we can enjoy the beauty of the garden. We can leave being busy for the bees, as we give first place of our time to The Master Gardener.

Put Your Pencils Down

Tests can be nerve wracking experiences. The second hand on the clock suddenly seems more important to you when you are in those tests that are timed. You may want to hurry, but you also want to answer every question the right way. It seems that there is so much at stake, and then you hear the words, "Put your pencils down."

The time is up. Your mind may race about those questions left unanswered, or the ones that you might have changed, but time has expired. This test is over. No more chances to altar your score. Now the only thing left to do is to wait.

Some tests in life will be more important than others. Perhaps you will take the SAT, PSAT, a military entrance test, or maybe the GRE. Of all the tests you can take in your life, there is one test your sure don't want to fail. This test has only one question – What will you do with Jesus?

You may choose an answer something like the following:

a. I agree with the philosophy of Jesus and, therefore I will probably go to heaven.
b. I hope my life has been good enough, and I hope to go to heaven.
c. There are many teachers, and I am not sure there is a heaven.

d. I know for sure that I will go to heaven because I have died to myself and received Christ, and now live for Him until that day arrives when I go to be with Him for eternity.

The funny thing about the life test is that you always wish there were more options. The not so funny thing is that this test is the most serious of your life and there are no other options. One more thing about this test is that it also is a timed test. Yes, there is a clock running, but only the Father in heaven is watching that second hand tick.

Matthew 24:42 says this:

"Watch therefore, for you do not know what hour your Lord is coming."

Every day we see the political heat rising again in the Middle East. The scene is being set. The time is short. Jesus is coming back.

I always knew when the teacher was headed back to her desk that she was about to announce that the time was up. When we see things heating up we know again the time in almost up. Maybe even today we will be going up to heaven.

How many questions do you left unanswered? How many people that you love will not be ready? Today is the day of salvation as tomorrow may be too late. There won't even be a second to hear, "Put your pencils down."

Side by Side

One Christmas season when I was about eleven, my little brother Bobby and I set out to buy our Christmas gifts together. These were not good days in our family. A divorce was on the horizon, and a good bit of yelling and things that one would not necessarily ascribe to the holiday season had become our everyday life. It still was Christmas, so together we went shopping for presents.

We began looking for something special and we pooled our limited funds so that we could buy the perfect gifts for those we loved. Our mother was on the top of our list. We really didn't have any good ideas as we scoped the shelves and hoped that something would stand out as the right gift for her. We had big hopes that the perfect gift would also be within our limited budget.

Suddenly there it was - a ceramic music box. It had an older sister with her arm around her little brother on the top of the box. It played the tune, "Side by Side." The words of that song tell of a time of low income, bad weather and storms of life, and yet these little ones on top could walk along and sing a song because they were together.

This is so like the members of the church which is the body of Christ. We so need each other. There are days of material plenty and days of plenty of storms. Yet, God has given us the gift of each other to bring life into true focus and meaning. We can celebrate the good together, and encourage and build up each other when times are hard. We all need to be reminded that God is good even when what we see in front of us does not look good at all.

Hebrews 10:23-25 reminds us of this very point:

"Let us hold fast the confession of our hope without wavering, for He who promised is faithful. And let us consider one another in order to stir up love and good works, not forsaking the assembling of ourselves together, as is the manner of some, but exhorting one another, and so much the more as you see the Day approaching."

Well, my brother and I had just enough money for that little music box. Our mother loved it and put it where everyone could see it. I believe she probably understood the meaning of that box more than we did at that time. Today, that box sits on my coffee table where everyone can see it. It still plays, and it continues to stir up the memory of how dear my brother was to me during those times that were so difficult and painful in my life.

Oh, one other thing that I still have is the lasting love and deep friendship of my younger brother. You see, though our mother is now in heaven, we are still those same children who are walking together, "Side by Side."

Baby Faith

With all Christians, there is the day that we become "born again" receiving, as Jesus told Nicodemus in John 3, a new birth, a new life, and a brand new way to live. This event begins the greatest season of change in any person's life. Change is not always easy, even change we desire, but this change, this transformation is completely for our benefit.

One change that comes early in this rebirth is a little item called "faith." Let's just call it "baby faith." We all exercise faith in our daily lives without realizing it. When we sit in a chair we have faith that it will hold us. When we work for someone we have faith that the proverbial check is in the mail. Baby faith is a little different. This is faith in God. Faith in what you cannot see and faith to do things that you lack the ability to accomplish.

Hebrews 11:1 describes this kind of faith:

"Now faith is the substance of things hoped for, the evidence of things not seen."

Early in my Christian walk, I encountered several things that challenged my "baby faith." In fact, they challenged a few other people too! I had just graduated from El Cerrito High School.

For many reasons, college was not an option for me at that time. I was seeking God for my future and needing much more than mere "baby faith."

Our home life could best be described as unstable. Fellowship in my weekly Bible study leveled the playing field for me each time I went. It was in this Bible study that I first heard of a church called *Calvary Chapel*. One of the members of the Bible study group filled me in on what God was doing in Southern California at that church. The problem for me was that I was currently living in Northern California. Suddenly I knew it! God wanted me to fly to Los Angeles! This was a big challenge for my "baby faith." It was the ravings of a lunatic, according to my mother.

I had enough money to buy a one way ticket to Los Angeles International Airport and fifty dollars left in my pocket. Just getting on that plane was a big step for my little "baby faith." Upon my arrival, I had to decide what I was going to do next. So, I found a phone booth and called the operator. I told her I was looking for Calvary Chapel. Before I knew it she connected me to the church and on the other end was a kind voice who responded to my story with, "You did what?"

Within a couple of hours I found myself in the care of the most wonderful congregation on earth! It was in this growing body of believers that I was provided the opportunity to get a firm foundation in the Word of God - The Holy Bible. This became the greatest blessing of my life.

Even more wonderful still, was that God had come through for me and built up my little "baby faith."

We all start with "baby faith" on the road to becoming a spiritual warrior for God. There is no microwave process or instant growth program. Instead, we grow in a process of prayer and trust as we encounter each challenge that is placed before us. Then, before we know it, we find we no longer are in the infancy of "baby faith" and moving on to lessons of greater faith.

VISA

Teenage life is filled with many "first" experiences. There is the first driver's license (I think I have seen some of those kids on the road), the first car (I often wonder who is paying for it), the first date (just too much to think about on that one), and the list goes on.

One of my "first" experiences was really a "one, two punch". Actually, it began with a good deal of fun. One afternoon, I picked up my mail and there it was - an application from VISA. The enclosed letter said I had been approved for my "first" credit card. Frankly, I should have known better. After all if I had been approved for the card why did I need the application? Yet, no such rational thought was going on in my mind at that moment.

Well, within a matter of weeks I had a little plastic card with my name on it. I had "The Power," and boy could I use it. Not long after, I picked up my mail and there *it* was - my first Visa bill. Oh no! Surely I could not have spent several hundred dollars! The minimum payment was not the $10 per month from the advertisement. No, it was much more and was really going to kill my little budget.

I had made a terrible mistake. Now, I was interested in reading all the fine print (a little late.) I found that if I paid the minimum payment that I was going to be paying for many, many more years. This couldn't be the best solution to my problem.

Then I thought of my eldest brother, a junior partner with the largest accounting firm in the United States. Since, in my mind, he made and astronomical income, he would be my salvation and help me pay my bill. Keep in mind that I was still a teenager with a hard lesson to learn.

Post haste I picked up the phone, called my brother, and told him my sad little story. He quietly listened on the other end of the line. Finally he said, "I am not going to pay your bill for you. You got yourself into this situation. The only way to be sure that you won't do this again is if you suffer the consequences of your poor choices."

It seemed I had two choices. Firstly, I could be angry with my brother for not being willing to rescue me (surely he would see I had been duped). Secondly, I could accept the truth of his words, suffer the correction, and pay the price for my choices. Option one could make me angry and bitter. Option two would really rescue me from future rotten decisions and fix accountability on me - right where it belonged.

Hebrews 12:6 gave me the direction I needed to choose rightly:

"For the Lord corrects and disciplines everyone whom He loves, and He punishes, even scourges, every son who He accepts and welcomes to His heart and cherishes."

It was not my brother offering me correction. No, it was my heavenly Father training and teaching me another hard lesson on the road of life. It was not a mean, angry Father either. This is the hand of a loving Father teaching us the lessons we need at the time we need them most.

I will freely admit that paying that bill was a struggle. There were many things I had do without to come up with the extra money to pay each month. And then it happened! One afternoon I went to pick up my mail and there it was - my billing statement from VISA. This time the balance was zero! This put one big smile on my face as I headed for the scissors and the trash can to say good-bye to VISA.

Philadelphia

W hen our children were very young I took the opportunity to home school them. The Army was often
sending my husband on many temporary duty assignments
(TDY) away from our home station. We never liked saying
good-bye to each other, and once in awhile, we went with
my husband on these trips.

When the kids were studying about Benjamin Franklin
and George Washington, my husband got orders for a TDY
trip to Philadelphia. Considering our recent studies, and the
value this trip might pose for our children, we accompanied
him on this trip. Philadelphia means "the city of brotherly
love." It comes from the root word *philia* in the Greek. This
means to have a loving bond and connection to each other.
Since I had already taught this to the kids, I had great hopes
for what the trip Philadelphia would hold in store for us.

We arrived in Philadelphia full of anticipation, and we
were shocked beyond belief. Downtown Philadelphia, while
full of history and relics of our country, was also full of home-
less people, drunks laying on the sidewalk, pan handlers and
other elements unfamiliar to our children. With a mother's
heart, I was frightened for the safety of our little ones in this
place. It was certainly not the place of brotherly love.

While visiting the United States Mint, we encountered a
fellow begging for money. My husband, unwilling to simply

hand him money offered to buy the poor fellow some lunch. We walked over to a street vendor selling the famous "Philly Cheese Steak" sandwiches and told the man to order whatever he wanted to eat. A very funny thing happened! The fellow said, "Hey Joe, give me the usual." What?

My husband was giving what we could share and suddenly we were feeling as if we were being taken for granted. How often did this guy do this? Then we realized, if Philadelphia didn't offer us brotherly love, maybe we could offer brotherly love to Philadelphia. Even if it meant being used.

Hebrews 13:1 says:

"Let brotherly love continue. Do not forget to entertain strangers, for by so doing some have unwittingly entertained angels."

Now, I don't know if the guy on that street was an angel. I don't always understand the motives of those I see seeking and reaching out to receive the charity from others. It really does not matter at all. What matters is what the motive is in our own hearts. There is only one motive acceptable - Love! I am sure God is hard at work on my life, ever seeking to give me a heart of Philadelphia.

See's Candy

L ife seems to always end up following the "Rule of Three." Have you ever noticed this?

For example, we have the Father, Son and Holy Spirit, the past, present and future, and honor code of West Point, "Duty, Honor, and Country." Even in engineering and architecture, the "rule of three" applies to design.

One of my personal trio's in life goes like this: Sweet, Swedish, and See's. This won't make any sense to most folks, but my Granny Weston was the sweetest person I have yet to meet this side of heaven. She came from good Swedish roots and the more I learn about the Swedes, the more I can see that she was the "real deal" on that score. The third item in this trio is a marvelous candy store called. "See's Candies."

All three came together in my young life. I would visit Granny, learn about our Swedish heritage, and then she would take me to the See's Candy Store near her home. Now See's Candies is a black and white shop. Filled with glass cases that are crystal clean, each case has tray upon tray of the sweetest confections on earth. No preservatives, no fillers, just all natural sweet goodness.

If it isn't already obvious to you, I just loved that candy shop. Granny was never one to indulge in quantity. So, I would have to choose two pieces of candy, be thankful, and leave the store without a single complaint. After all, Granny said that was what Swedish children did. No exceptions to that rule, and I never challenged it either.

When I became an adult, I found that I could go to See's anytime I wanted. I could buy any amount that I could afford. I could even complain out loud if I desired to do so. It seems like another rule of three has just exposed itself.

Soon my bathroom scale began to indicate the number of unaccompanied trips to the candy store. See's, instead of being my sweet friend, suddenly was not so sweet. My love for that candy is probably as much an emotional connection to my Granny as it is sweet to my taste buds. None the less, my visits to See's became a habit that was out of control, and The Holy Bible calls that sin.

Hebrews 12:1 tells us what to do with just such a habit:

"Therefore we also, since we are surrounded by so great a cloud of witnesses, let us **lay aside every weight, and the** *sin which so easily ensnares us,* **and let us run with endurance the race that is set before us**" (emphasis added).

It is clear that we all have an area of sin that easily ensnares us. Sometimes it can be in the area of something we eat. The Bible says we need to lay the "it" aside so we can run this Christian race. To do that, we will have to endure the nasty temper tantrums of our flesh, while it learns to submit to discipline. When we come to Christ, we agree to lay **all** sin aside to enter the race. Today I can visit See's without a problem. I have gone back to the days of my Swedish Grandmother's rules, get only two pieces, and go home without complaint, making a candy store visit worth the wait.

Welcome Home

I was born and raised in what is referred to as "The Bay Area" of northern California for 13 years. I love my home state. In fact, at the end of every family vacation, we would all sing "California Here I Come" as we drove back across the state line heading for home. I especially like the words: *Sunkist maid says, "Don't be late." That's why I can hardly wait. Open up your Golden Gate — California, USA!* This family tradition left its mark on me as, at the end of every vacation, no matter how nice the trip, "I can hardly wait" to come home again.

At the age of thirteen, my parents divorced and within a matter of weeks, I moved with two brothers and my mother to live in North Carolina. We were going to live near our cousins and my mother's extended family. Nothing could have prepared me for this culture shock!

I did not dress like my cousins. I didn't speak the same way people spoke in North Carolina.

Everything had to change and was changing all at once. Frankly, clothes are just clothes and I even tried faking a southern accent to fit in. There was one change I just could never make - fitting into "clicks." We did not have "clicks" in California. I really thought it was stupid to think anyone was better than anyone else simply based on income and address. What was wrong with these people anyway?

In San Francisco, businessmen in fine suits would strike up conversations with people who were poorly dressed on the street. Not so in North Carolina. There everyone was cast in a group and only in that group were you allowed to function. Anyone with the audacity to challenge these social norms was "out cast" and I remember the word "slime" being used to label these people. Outrageous! I was sure that the word "slime" should never be used when referring to a person.

Soon, it was perfectly clear that I was no Southerner, and I was going to have a pretty rough ride during my time in North Carolina. When I became a Christian two years later, I began to see my new faith challenging my thinking. As I grew in Christ, many ideas had to change. One day, the subject of showing partiality finally came up. You can imagine my complete surprise to find that God thought just like I did - at least on this one subject.

James 2:1 - 4 says this:

"My brethren, do not hold the faith of our Lord Jesus Christ, the Lord of glory, with partiality. For if there should come into your assembly a man with gold rings, in fine apparel, and there should also come in a poor man in filthy clothes, and you pay attention to the one wearing the fine clothes and say to him, 'You sit here in a good place,' and say to the poor man, 'You stand there,' or, 'Sit here at my footstool,' have you not shown partiality among yourselves, and become judges with evil thoughts?"

California may have a reputation for some nutty ideas but the idea of treating all people with dignity and respect, no matter their financial status or clothing designer, rates high with God and man. This way of thinking should not be isolated to one state or another it is rather the way that God would have us think no matter which state we live in.

Though this life is seldom thought of as a vacation, it is still true that it is not our final destination. And when we head to our real home one day I won't be surprised to hear some music along the way! If someone is singing something that sounds like the California State Song don't worry – It will probably just be me!

Lost Treasures

While walking on the beach of Coronado Island, I was taking in all the scenery, enjoying the wet soft sand between my toes, and seeking out little living things in the tidal pools along the shore. The previous night there had been a wedding on the beach. We watched the joyous bride and groom while they posed for pictures, and we laughed as they laughed. It seems that joy is contagious.

I was thinking about the number of weddings that have taken place on that beach. During my walk, I noticed a fellow with a metal detector seeking items of value and lost treasure in the sand. I wondered what sort of lost treasure he finds every day as he diligently combs the beach. Could it be lost wedding rings, as that could easily happen at any beach? Could it be he finds lost gold coins from pirate ships of the past? I am sure he finds current coinage as well. One thing for sure, he had his head down and continually moved up and down the beach. This was serious business.

God is like that too. After the sin of Adam in the Garden of Eden, God came seeking His lost son. Can you hear Him calling, "Adam, where are you?" The broken hearted cry of the Father was reaching out to the one who had gone astray – who was lost. Jesus is like this too! The Bible says, "For the Son of Man has come to seek to save that which was lost." Jesus gave everything to seek and save us. The Holy Spirit is like that too!

In James 4:5 we read, "The Spirit who dwells in us yearns jealously."

He yearns because we cultivate everything but our relationship with God. Yearning for us to leave the friendship of the world, the Holy Spirit desires that we seek to be the friend of God.

A loving relationship with God seems to be worth so much more than lost jewelry or gold coins on a lovely beach. We are His lost treasure and His seeking for us is a demonstration of His love. Our response should always be just like the joy of that bride and groom at the wedding - contagious joy. Joy? Yes, joy because we are His treasure that was once lost.

Seeking shells on the beach,
Or golden coins in sand beneath
Hidden jewels from those who've come before
To walk upon that lovely shore.

Seeking, Seeking a worthy find
Of something precious left behind
Seeking such a valued treasure
That brings the seeker more than pleasure.

This is the joy God has in you
He gave what no earthy man would do
So willing to endure the cost
To know the thrill of finding what was lost.

The Death of the Pelican

During the celebration of our twenty-fifth wedding anniversary, my husband and I enjoyed the beaches of Aruba. Every culture in every new place can be so captivating. The hotel was lovely, but their prices for coffee were more debilitating than captivating for our budget. It was time to go investigate options on the beach for coffee at a better price.

I sure am thankful for that excursion. Even though the prices drove us on that morning walk, it turned out to provide us not only with coffee but also a very interesting experience. Not very far down the beach was a little, very old, pier. Residing on that pier was a wonderful tiny coffee bar with some of the tastiest pastry and most delicious smoothies I have ever sampled.

The name of this part of the beach is called Pelicans' Point. Sitting at a table adjacent to the pier we enjoyed our breakfast. At the same time, we were entertained by the "morning show" provided by the local pelicans diving for their own breakfast.

The proprietor of the coffee bar started a conversation with us as he noticed our intent interest in the pelicans. He explained to us the supposed life cycle of a pelican. According to our "guide" it seems they fish by dive bombing all their lives. Though the habits of the pelicans are interesting, it is even more interesting how a pelican dies. It seems they damage their eyes in their endless dive bombing and when they are old their eyes wear out from their fishing and they finally die of starvation.

My husband later found out doing some research on the Internet that pelicans really do not go blind in their fishing process. Nonetheless, the story does provide a metaphor to a life lesson. You see, the Lord has called us all to be "fishers of men." Matthew 4:19 says: "Then He (Jesus) said to them, 'Follow Me, and I will make you fishers of men.'"

Just like the hunger of the pelican, we cannot be satisfied unless we feed the need of our hearts to follow Jesus and become fishers also - fishers of men. Also like the pelican, we are to seek and dive with a passion, earnestly seeking to save that which was lost. For us, it is not only to meet our needs but to meet the needs of others and glorify God.

In the end we will face death, human and pelican alike. As humans we are given the opportunity to do or not to do what God has created us for – fishing for men and women who have a desire to live for Jesus. I think God also made the pelican to teach us that satisfaction is only ever found in serving the purpose of your creation. Materials things wear out, fashion changes like the wind, and vocations come and go with scarcely a person recalling your name.

No, only serving God and serving others in the fishing cycle will bring you to discover the purpose for which God created you. Maybe the death of the pelican is God's lesson to teach us how we should live.

Be Good

There is that old saying, "when the cat's away, the mice will play." Most likely every parent has said that to their own children at one time or another. It was sure a true saying in our home.

While we were with our children they were very well behaved. In fact, looking back I'm not sure who was in the Army, my husband or the kids and me. Even so they sure were great kids.

But - don't you hate that word? Our children were extraordinarily good, but they could really be hard on their baby sitters. When we were going out, we would always say, "Be good." This little saying was accompanied with a promise and also a threat. If they were "good" there would be a reward. If they were "naughty" there would be another kind of reward. As we left they would smile and promise that this time they would "be good."

It seemed no matter who we had as a sitter, we always came home to some long description of every naughty thing they had come up with while we were out. Then we were forced to fulfill on our promises. Sadly, we had to keep our word and deliver discipline where it was called for.

The apostle Peter wrote something that best describes this scenario. Peter knows he will soon die for his faith and is leaving his last words for the body of Christ. Also it is much more than Peter expressing his direction to the body of Christ. Rather, it is God through Peter giving us our instructions.

"But also for this very reason, giving all diligence, add to your faith virtue, to virtue knowledge, to knowledge self control, perseverance, to perseverance godliness, to godliness brotherly kindness, to kindness love" (2 Peter 5-7).

Virtue means to "be good." Isn't that interesting? God is telling us to "be good." Knowledge encourages us to continue learning about His word. Self control tells us to put our flesh on notice to "behave." Perseverance helps us understand that we must stay the course. Godliness means act just like God would in your situations. Kindness is how we are to treat one another.

Love means to do love to others without needing to be loved back. Love is never optional for the Christian.

This sounds like a good list of instructions for any child even if it is for the child of God. One day we did finally find a terrific baby-sitter. Her name was Lena Palella. We said everything we always said as we went out that evening. I recall praying more for this sweet Italian grandmother than for our children as we left the house. The good news is that when we returned home we found that our little ones had become the Little "Army Angels" that we knew that they could be. Then we were finally able to give our little ones blessings! What a joy that was for us. Oh, we gave Lena the biggest blessing - a good tip!

We no longer need Lena's services as our children have grown up. Since we are all God's kids, we do have a sitter to help us while we wait for Jesus to return. That helper is the Holy Spirit. He is there to help us all to remember to "be good" and that obedience brings blessings and sin brings consequences – so "be good!"

Ancient Lessons

New and improved are the mantra of the marketing world. Vendors market goods and services, tantalizing buyers to sample their products. The older I get, the more I understand that what is "New" is really "Old." What is "Hot" will soon be not. What you buy today may end up in a garage sale tomorrow. This is also true when it comes to fashion. The clothing most recently on the shelves has the styles that I can easily recall from my younger days.

Apparently Solomon shared this feeling as he said in Ecclesiastes 1:10:

"Is there anything of which it may be said, 'See, this is new?'"

This truth also applies to fashionable behavior. In the 1920s, it was in vogue to leave the farms and head for city life. What was left behind was so much more than the farm. When the young people left their homes, they also left the teachings from the Bible. They were seeking something new.

Now, once again, we are called back to the ancient lessons that will encourage, bless, and change our world. Not all the old lessons are easy to learn. Maybe this is why it was so easy for those who went before us to leave them, to drift away as the writer of the Book of Hebrews warns in chapter two.

The ancient lesson for us today is found in 2 Peter 2:4-6:

"For if God did not spare the angels who sinned, but cast them down to hell and delivered them into chains of darkness, to be reserved for judgment; and did not spare the ancient world, but saved Noah, one of eight people, a preacher of righteousness, bringing in the flood on the world of the ungodly; and turning the cities of Sodom and Gomorrah into ashes, condemned them to destruction, making them an example to those who would live ungodly."

The ancient lessons are all good. The thing that determines if we are blessed or cursed is the thing that has always determined everyone's future — our choices.

Ancient Lessons for my good,
Teach me to do the things I should.
Ancient Lessons train my mind,
And help me to leave my sins behind.

Ancient lesson we should all be keeping,
And submit to lessons God is teaching.

Ancient Lessons, I don't think so.

Shake, Rattle, and Go

Another earthquake hit California this week. These shaking quakes affect far more than land mass. They disrupt daily activities; shake up people with the knowledge of how fragile life is and how soon it may all be over. It so happens that we had just left California a couple days before this last quake hit. Once again we were reminded that life is a daily journey of events that are beyond our control.

Speaking of a journey, we arrived at the airport with all the required preparations before we could board the plane. You know the routine: security checks, tickets checks, and personal identity checks. None of the above was difficult, but still they had to be done before you could proceed to the plane.

Finally, we arrived at the gate and waited for our section to be called to board. Boarding pass in hand, passport out and carry on items in tow. We were ready to go. On board and all bags stowed we buckled up and waited on the control tower to give our pilot the go ahead for takeoff.

2 Peter 3:10-12 tells us about another kind of takeoff:

"But the day of the Lord will come as a thief in the night, in which the heavens will pass away with a great noise, and the elements will melt with fervent heat; both the earth and the works that are in it will be burned up. Therefore, since all these things will be dissolved, what manner of persons ought you to be in holy conduct and godliness, looking for and hastening the coming of the day of God?"

Just like preparations taken in earthquake zones, or checks before a flight, we are encouraged to be even more ready for the coming of the Lord.

There have been many flights that I had to wait on the runway quite awhile for my plane to takeoff, but I was always ready. The next time on a runway you have to wait, or the next time

The ground beneath your feet begins to shake may it remind you that you alone have the choice to make for your final destination.

Sooner than any of us might imagine the voice from God's tower will be telling Jesus it is finally time for us to go, and the Scripture tells us that "those who were ready went in"(Matthew 25:10). Amen!

Summer Trips

Summer time is often a time of sun, fun and also vacations. Vacations carry us off to locations that are filled with interesting attractions, but the locations may also be filled with different ways of living.

Recently we vacationed in San Diego. We landed to a cool 66 degrees and a lovely breeze. Now, that is some change from South Carolina 90's and high humidity. So, the weather though different was very good. Oh, but how quickly I missed the hospitality and manners that we enjoy in the South. No doors were held open there in lovely California, and there were no "yes ma'am" or "no sir" either. When we said "please and thank you" people looked at us in an odd way. I imagine that they were wondering what planet we had just come from. Then to top it off, they never serve "Sweet Tea."

Sweet Tea must be one of the best known icons of the South. Forget the palmetto tree or NASCAR racing, sweet tea will linger on your mind long after your glass is empty. In the book of I John, chapter three, John also tells us something about a different way of life.

"And now, little children, abide in Him, that when He appears, we may have confidence and not be ashamed before Him at His coming. If you know that He is righteous, you know that everyone who practices righteousness is born of Him" (I John 3:28-29).

Just as we change our manner of living when we vacation we also change our lifestyle and manners when we submit our lives to Christ. The word "righteous" just means to live the "right way." Before we knew Christ, we lived in this world going our own way - the wrong way. Now, having come to Christ, we have been told to submit to Christ and live a new way - the right way.

We are told now to abide (live) in Him. Then we are told to practice living the new way. This is why early Christians were called "The Way." They were so named by non-Christians who clearly saw the "new way" that these Christians were living.

Thank God that this is not just a vacation or some "trip." Vacations never last, and as sweet as the tea is in the South, it will never compare to the sweetness we now enjoy with our fellowship in Him and with each other. This sweetness lasts long after church is over and lingers in our hearts even when we return to our homes.

Finally, after a vacation we come home. It is always good to come home too! There will also be the day we come home to heaven which is really our home town anyway.

This is a Test

Love suffers long
Love is kind
Love does not envy
Love does not parade itself
Love is not puffed up
Love is not rude
Love does not seek its own
Love is not provoked
Love thinks no evil
Love does not rejoice in iniquity
Love rejoices in truth
Love bears all things
Love hopes all things
Love believes all things
Love endures all things
I Corinthians 13: 4-7

Back in chapter 11, Paul told us to examine ourselves. This chapter gives us a great opportunity to do that. Take this passage and whenever it says "love" insert your name instead. For example, Susan suffers long and is kind. Susan does not envy, and Susan does not think evil. Susan never fails. Go ahead and take the test! How did you do?

Jesus suffers long and is kind, Jesus does not envy, and Jesus isn't provoked. Jesus never fails.

This is a great test. See how far you can get down the road of what the Lord would have you to be. This is describing what God wants us to be. He wants His love to be operating in our lives. God ahead and examine yourself. I hope you pass the test.

How Is Your Aim

Many years ago I took a shot at archery. No pun intended. I bought a pretty bow and thought this was going to be a lot of fun. When I went out for the first time (thank God I had a teacher),

I followed the instruction and WANG! The arrow flew off the bow, but the arrow didn't hit the target. Worse than missing the target, the string hit my arm. Wow, I had quite a welt!

You see, I had a bow, a teacher, and knowledge of this sport, yet there were still some things about aiming and hitting the target that I was missing – again no pun intended.

Well, what about my aim? My aim improved with a few more lessons. I had fewer welts too and I learned to release the arrows without having the bow string recoil on my forearm. I also learned an important lesson that I had heard many times before – we only hit what we aim for.

The applicable Scripture for this life lesson is Psalms 17:3.

"I have purposed (aimed) that my mouth shall not transgress (sin.)" This is a very good goal to shoot for because Jesus said, "it is not that which goes into the mouth that defiles a man, but that which comes out" (Mark 7:15).

The first time you try to purpose not to sin, do not be surprised if the words you have chosen not to use still try to come out of your mouth all by themselves. Up until now, you might have believed that you were in control of your words and used them as you desired. Now the shock of reality is that the words seem to have you!

Tricky little devils aren't they? They really have asserted control, but they do not really have control. The Bible says, "whom the Son sets free is free indeed." So, assert your free will and resist the urge to sin with your mouth. You will be amazed to find those rotten words, comments, and the rest of your offensive speech no longer has a hold on you. Now you will be hitting the target and not getting any welts in the process.

Dismissed

Elementary schools have different bells to signal different times in a school day. There is one bell to begin class, one bell for recess, one bell for lunch, and one bell for the rotation of classes.

Perhaps the best bell is the one that sounds dismissal.

When I was in school, I knew every bell and what it meant. Like most children, I really liked the recess bell and lunch bell. My favorite bell was the dismissal bell. I can remember sitting twisting in my seat, watching the big clock on the wall and knowing that bell was just about to go off. Then eureka, it would sound and off we would all go to the joys of a free afternoon with our friends.

This reminds me of our present time here on the earth. God made the earth. Genesis 1:1 states, "In the beginning God created the heavens and the earth." This was like the bell that said class was about to begin. There were 400 years of silence between the Old and New Testaments which seems like recess to me. Then Jesus came and started the clock ticking again. Our next bell will be a trumpet sounding for those in Christ to come up to be with Him, before the great tribulation visits the earth to try the sons of men.

Certainly everyone who loves the Lord is looking forward to that trumpet. There is sadness, however, that will come with that trumpet. It is dismissal. We will be lifted out of the earth and our time on earth to serve God will be over. There will be no more time to share our faith with those who are lost. There will not be one more second to express our appreciation in a life of service to Christ because that time on the earth for us will be over. Class, as we know, it will come to an end. All those that we didn't share our faith with will be left without faith.

It is an interesting dilemma. How can I be excited and joyful for the trumpet coming to rescue me when there are so many that we have failed to tell the Good News? Revelation 4:6 gives us a glimpse of heaven on that great day:

"Before the throne there was a sea of glass, like crystal. And in the midst of the throne and round the throne were four living creatures full of eyes in front and in back. The first living creature was like a lion, the second living creature like a calf, the third living creature had a face like a man, and the fourth living creature was like a flying eagle. The four living creatures, each having six wings, were full of eyes around and within. And they do not rest day or night saying:

'Holy, holy, holy, Lord God Almighty, who was and is and is to come.'"

According to these verses even the most amazing creatures will be spending their time declaring the Holiness, Power and Coming of Jesus. Perhaps they are the example to us who are sitting in our seats, probably twisting and some even clock watching getting ready for the bell. This is the way to have real joy as we wait for His coming. This is our time to tell the world about God's Holiness, Power and that He is coming soon. We may even see some receive Christ and be ready for that trumpet just as we are. Then we can hear that great trumpet and know that we have used our time wisely before class is dismissed.

Better Than Tupperware

In my early days of married life I found great fun and fellowship with other ladies while attending Tupperware Parties. Now Tupperware was and probably still is a super product but the social aspect of the party was the big draw for me. It was while attending these parties that I gained some good cooking ideas and some better money saving ideas as well. You see Tupperware has a product to maximize the shelf life or refrigerator life of costly produce and other grocery items.

Though the parties were plentiful, my budget was not. So, I would buy one piece of Tupperware at each party. Based on what I saw, the other young wives were ordering in a similar way. I could see my situation was not the only tight budget in the house. It did not take too long, however, before I had a bread keeper, a bacon keeper, an ice cream keeper and the list goes on and on. Each product did the job well and I even still have some of the early pieces that I bought a long ago.

What sort of keeper do we have for mankind? This is a problem that even Tupperware cannot fix. We all seem to face loss, grief, and even come up against those who would harm us for no earthly reason. Some people seem to be mean and hurtful because they derive some sick pleasure from it. Where do we turn when there is no where left to turn? Where shall we run when we are all run out?

Psalm 121 answers the questions:

"I will lift up my eyes to the hills from whence comes my help? My help comes from the LORD, who made heaven and earth. He will not allow your foot to be moved; He who keeps you will not slumber. Behold, He who keeps Israel shall neither slumber nor sleep. The LORD is your keeper; The LORD is your shade at your right hand. The sun shall not strike you by day or the moon by night. The LORD shall preserve you from all evil; He shall preserve your soul.

The LORD shall preserve your going out and your coming in from this time forth and even forevermore."

Now that's what I call a keeper! Tupperware can only extend and preserve the grocery items it held. Yet, when God keeps you, will be preserved forever. No party to attend, no budget required, the God in whose hand is your very breath is keeping you. This is a great promise for the child of God. You see this promise does not apply to those outside of Christ. In Christ I am His and He is mine and then He keeps me all the time-no Tupperware required.

Puzzling Words

The more time I spend with people, the more I find how similar we are. Oh, there may be a little difference in the packaging, but it seems we all have very similar temptations, desires, and physical characteristics. There is one little physical characteristic that at the moment comes to mind – the tongue.

My parents loved to do crossword puzzles. In fact, every morning before my father would leave for work he would work the newspaper puzzle with my mother. It was at that table with them that I heard many interesting sounding words. That does not mean I knew what those words meant.

Early one morning, I went to visit an elderly lady who lived up the street. I really never thought I was doing her any favor as I enjoyed our visits. I overheard her speaking with another neighbor as I walked up her drive. They were discussing another neighbor, another similarity in people. At the end of their discussion I interjected that the reason for the neighbor's issues was because our neighbor was a plutocrat. Both women looked at me with dismay and I quickly decided that I'd better hurry home. Later that day, I heard the phone ring and then my mother had a little discussion with me about using words that I didn't fully understand.

What could I understand - I was six!

It turns out my little lesson on speech has something in common in the lives of many people in history. In Psalm 141 King David had a tongue problem as well. He also had a cure my mother never told me about.

"Set a guard, O LORD over my mouth.
Keep watch over the door of my lips.
Do not incline my heart to any evil thing,
To practice wicked works." (Psalm 141:3 -4)

My mother was great at teaching me what not to say, but I needed to know how to control my mouth. Try as I might I would still say the wrong thing at times. Try as she might to discipline me for any wrong statement, the results were never long lived.

Finally one day I discovered Jesus! No, finally one day Jesus found me. I learned that I was not alone with tongue problems. I found others in the Bible with similar struggles. The remedy for the "foot in mouth" disease is also found within those holy pages. It is asking God to be my help and change the desires of my heart. You see when wrong words come out of my mouth they didn't originate there. Those rotten reoccurring words come from the abundance of my heart.

But, when I ask God to change that heart and submit my will to obey Him the result is a new heart.

My Mother is no longer around to whip my tongue into shape, now I have God who will even put a guard at my mouth, watch over my lips, and if need be He can become my muzzle and end the problem with words that puzzle.

First

Children have an affinity for wanting to be first. I suspect we who are adults want to be first as well: first in line, first to receive praise, first to receive the promotion, and first to get the trophy. As adults we are supposed to know better than to demand to be first or throw a tantrum to be first.

A commonly used word for first these days is priority. Many companies use professional trainers and mentors to help their employees get a handle on their work priorities. Priority is just saying what I do prior to other things. Priority is supposed to signify value and significance.

For the Christian, Jesus should always be in first place. It is obedience to His Word that shows He is in first place. In fact He said this, "If a man love me, he will keep my words and my Father will love him, and we will come unto him and make our abode with him" (John 14:23).

You might go so far as to say that Christian living is intended to be our first priority. Verse 24 says more, "He that does not love me does not keep my sayings."

To love Him is to obey Him. Not to love Him is not to obey Him. Sounds pretty clear what my priority should be. God help us all today to live our lives in such a way that shows that we live what we say by putting Jesus first.

Hiding

When our eldest son was two he really pulled a trick on my mother. She was visiting us for the week and was watching him while I was out on an errand. My husband was busy with yard work and all seemed in order. At least that was the way it was until my mother realized that my son was gone!

She told me that her first thought was that I would kill her. Then she got my husband and the frantic search began for the missing child. Our neighborhood was new and there were many open holes for sewer connections and the like that could pose a very great danger to a child.

Within a short period of time, all our neighbors joined the search party. Moving slowly through the tall grass at the end of the cul-de-sac their early search was uneventful.

My mother decided to go back to the house thinking that I would soon be there and she would tell me about the ordeal. When she got back to the house she decided to search one more time for our son. I can only imagine her calling his name - Michael. Thank God - there he was sitting in his closet, hiding. She told me that he had the cutest smile on his face and said "I tricked you! I was hiding." Isn't it amazing? One moment you can be terrified that the child has died and once the little stinker has been found you may be sure you are going to kill him yourself!

Life, like my old neighborhood, has many perils to be sure. We can be so like my son, playing one game or another and not being where we are supposed to be. Now, God, like my family and neighbors, does hunt for us. It is not that He does not know where we are. It is more that He is seeking a way into hardened hearts that have gone away from Him.

Psalm 145:18-20 says this:

"The LORD is near to all who call upon Him,
To all who call in truth,
He will fulfill the desire of those who fear Him,
He also will hear their cry and save them.
The LORD preserves all who love Him,
But, the wicked He will destroy"

I am told a great shout went up when little Michael was found. It was a great joy and quite a relief to all who were searching for him. For you see the moment he answered the call of my mother's voice he was found. Whenever we hide from God, He is as close to us as our will to call upon Him. The moment we call and admit the truth that has separated us from Him He is right there with us.

Now, Michael tells me that he was pretty sure he was going to get in trouble for what he did.

There are always consequences to our poor choices. There are also consequences when we hide from God, but staying lost is never the right answer.

When I came home that evening the entire mess was over. There was only the story to tell and the son restored to the family who loved him. Are you hiding? I hope not.

Benefits Package

Many years ago I landed my first full-time job. I was nervous, excited and oh yes, thrilled that I actually got the job. My first day was not what I had expected. I thought that I would go straight to my work station and begin as they say to "cut the mustard" and work. Instead, there was new employee orientation and my assignment was to spend several days with the human resources department. We would first learn as new employees the expectations of behavior and performance. We would also learn about our benefits package.

I had already agreed to the pay that I was offered, so I was amazed that there was going to be more to this job than work and pay. What a joy it was to learn that there were so many benefits with my new job. Here I was happy as could be to have a job and now my job had exceeded my hopes by providing more benefits than I had ever imagined.

God is just like this too! Broken and bruised from this world and our own poor choices (sins), we come to Jesus with joy and delight. We discover that He paid the price for us and granted us a relationship with Him, peace with God the Father, and to top it off, eternal life.

But, wait! You now have your entire lifetime to spend in God's HR department – reading and relating to Him in his precious Word, The Holy Bible.

Psalm 146:5-9 gives an outline of just a few of our new benefits:

"Happy is he who has the God of Jacob for his help, whose hope is in the LORD his God. Who made heaven and earth, the sea and all that is in them; Who keeps truth forever, who executes justice for the oppressed, who gives food to the hungry. The LORD gives freedom to the prisoners. The LORD opens the eyes of the blind; The LORD raises those who are bowed down; The LORD loves the righteous. The LORD watches over the strangers, He relieves the fatherless and widow; but the way of the wicked He turns upside down."

Psalm 103:2 says this:

"Bless The LORD, O my soul;
And forget not all His benefits."

Coming to Jesus has been a wonder. Coming to know Him has been even more than wonderful.

To think that God has provided so many wonderful things to bless us is more than I could have ever imagined. Now that's what I call a benefits package!

The Blowing of a Trumpet

Many years ago, my husband and I went to visit my Aunt Jane in North Carolina. The visit was even more special because my cousins and their husbands were also visiting. We were all young married couples and had so much in common with each other.

My youngest cousin and her husband especially made a connection with my husband and me. In our conversation we learned that both of our husbands loved to play the trumpet. This news sent the two men on a treasure hunt through my Aunt's basement seeking an old trumpet to play.

After a lovely luncheon and long conversations about the second coming of Christ several of my cousins went to take a nap. One of the young men was a new minister, and he was one who decided this was a good time to rest. All the while the two trumpet masters were still in search of the old family trumpet in the basement. Unknown to all of us the guys found that old trumpet. With a heart not to disturb anyone they went to the far corner of the basement to try out their musical skills. It turns out that the corner of the basement they choose was exactly below the bedroom of the young minister.

With all their young enthusiasm, they took turns blowing that trumpet. The poor minister woke with such a start! He sat straight up! Again the trumpet blew! He was now certain that it was none other than the Trumpet of God sounding to rapture the Church to be with Christ. Then the thought struck him - he wasn't going anywhere? Still sitting up in that bed he was convinced that he had been left behind. With panic, he ran to the other end of the house to see if anyone else had been left as well.

Well, there we were, all sitting around the table. The poor fellow white as a ghost told us the story. In that very moment the two young men emerged from the basement with the treasured trumpet! I am sure, if it were not for concern for my elderly Aunt, the young minister would have throttled those laughing young men.

There is humor in this story, but stark reality as well. You see, as I am writing, in two weeks there is coming the Feast of Trumpets. In Leviticus 23:23-25, The Jewish people had several feasts and all were fulfilled with one exception -the feast of trumpets and the feast of Tabernacles. The Jewish people used the trumpet to gather the people. Each year as we near this feast I cannot help but wonder if this is the time that God will blow that trumpet and call us home.

For the young minister there was great relief that he was not late or lost or left behind. Unfortunately when the trumpet of God sounds, many will be left behind. Today there is still time. God has provided another chance to escape and be with Him.

"Now this I say, brethren, that flesh and blood cannot inherit the kingdom of God; nor does corruption inherit incorruption. Behold, I tell you a mystery; we shall not all sleep (die), but we shall all be changed — in a moment, in the twinkling of an eye, at the last trumpet. For a trumpet will sound, and the dead will be raised incorruptible, and we shall be changed, this corruption must put on incorruption, and this mortal must put on immortality" (I Cor. 15: 50-54).

Panic

Prior to 1837, there was wide spread construction and industrial growth here in the United States.

The construction was mostly commercial and the price for that construction was paid in paper notes not in hard currency like gold or silver. Eventually things got so out of control that our government had to put a stop to these extravagant notes and thus came the financial panic of 1837. The woes of that panic of course affected the nation. We can see how it affected people by taking a more compelling look into the lives of those who actually lived through it.

One such person was Anna B. Warner. She was a young teenager in a wealthy home in New York City. She and her sister Susan were being raised by their father and an aunt after the death of their mother. In the panic, their father (Henry Warner) lost more than his money. Unable to cope with the pressure and his financial losses he withdrew into a deep depression and thus was of no earthly use to his little family. With what little reasoning capacity he had left, he sold most of their earthly possessions and moved to an island in the middle of the Hudson River. This island was called Constitution Island. It was there that they owned a summer house and there they would come to spend the rest of their lives.

231

It was on Constitution Island that Susan and Anna put their trust in Christ. It was there that God met their every need. I did not say that He met their every want. In the solitude of that island, these young ladies wrote over 100 books. Though you may not have heard of them before, I expect you have enjoyed one of their efforts all the same. As it was also on the island that Anna composed the hymn "Jesus Loves Me."

There have been many panics that have come and gone since 1837. There have been times of speculation and poor judgment. In all of these times, there is a golden window of opportunity. The opportunity is to use the pressure of those days to put our hearts and lives right with God and let Him use these panics for our good.

Psalm 46:4-5 says:

"There is a river whose streams shall make glad the city of God,
The holy place of the tabernacle of the Most High,
God is in the midst of her; she shall not be moved;
God will help her, just at the break of dawn."

When times get hard we can run and panic or we can run to the Lord. It is comforting to know that whether times are good or bad, it does not change the love and care that Jesus has for us.

The words that Anna penned bring peace to our hearts today just as they did for her those many years ago:

Jesus loves me, this I know,
For the Bible tells me so.
Little ones to Him belong,
They are weak, but He is strong.

Yes, Jesus loves me, yes Jesus loves me, yes Jesus Love me - the Bible tells me so.

May you find your help today in Jesus.

May He be in the midst of you and give you rest in whatever panic comes your way.

May He be the river that refreshes your soul when the rivers of life are out of control.

May we all learn from Anna and Susan Warner to always remember that Jesus loves us all.

Payday

The world of childhood is so wonderful and uncompli-cated. Children seldom think of where money comes from as evidenced by their confusion when they cannot have everything their heart's desire.

I recall when our youngest child was about three-years-old and wanted something she saw at the store. At the time, I told her that I did not have the money right now. She said, "That's okay Mommy, just use the card."

I would venture a guess that my child was not the first little person to associate the purchasing power of a credit card with her daily wants. This particular thought is not limited to childhood. It is important to grow up and learn that it requires money to pay those plastic cards off once you buy on impulse. Needless to say, we did not buy the item that day.

Another parallel with the ways of the world of money is with work and paychecks. I also recall learning about this process when I got my first job. I didn't know how long it would take to get paid. So, when I didn't get a check for two weeks I was outraged. Imagine I worked for two weeks before I actually got money. Well this is how we learn - right?

There is one other payday issue worth learning. This is the payday in God's economy. It requires much more than two weeks as God will be settling up the earnings of a lifetime. God's timing is not delinquent. It is instead patient, just, reasonable, and perfect. He has waited to settle much longer than I would have waited myself. However, it has been during the wait that I have learned the value of His perfect timing.

One last thing about God's timing is that some have taken His patience for lack of performance. Oh, not so. There is a payday coming! It would seem to some that God does not see, care, or may even approve of their disobedience to His Word. This is not true!

Revelation 11:18 says:

"The nations were angry, and Your wrath has come,
And the time of the dead, that they should be judged,
And that You should reward Your servants the prophets and the saints,
And those who fear Your name, small and great,
And should destroy those who destroy the earth."

As long-suffering as God is, His wrath will be equal to His mercy. His reward is coming with Him. For some it will be eternal bliss, and for others it will be wrath such as the world has never known. To some it will be the Great and Terrible Day of The Lord. To some it will just be a day of bestowing rewards and blessings, like payday.

The setting of the stage is so ready for the opening act of this play. Time has almost run out. The players are in their places. Before you know it, the proverbial check is in the mail. I would say, it could very well happen today, that you will receive your payday.

Playing with Snakes

Growing up in Northern California in the 50's was a good bit different from growing up today in most parts of America. In the days of my youth, parents did not have to entertain their children. Nor were they under their feet during the day. Instead, the children were ushered out the door to play in the yard. As they grew older, the boundary of the yard extended to ball field, play grounds, and the local woods.

Toys were not at *Toys R Us*. In fact major toy outlets did not exist. No, our toys were the ones provided by childhood invention and also whatever nature provided that looked interesting. We played games like: Hop Scotch, Kick the Can (usually using some old coffee can), Four Square, Jump Rope, and Hide and Seek. The natural toys were: catching bees, catching frogs, using butterfly nets and oh yes, catching snakes. SNAKES! Yes, snakes.

California has plenty of snakes both of the non-venomous and venomous varieties. Parents gave long lectures about the distinguishing characteristics between those snakes that posed dangers and those that were safe to handle. Red on yellow friendly fellow, for example, is the California King Snake. Black on the yellow this snake could kill a fellow reminded us of the coral snake. Snakes with a diamond head could leave a child dead also helped us keep away from the poisonous snakes – well was supposed to keep us away.

Of course we tried to follow these rules, but one thing about catching snakes is that you seldom get close enough to check out the head until you actually catch them. Now the coral snake you can easily identify from a distance, so no problem there.

One summer day my middle brother caught an unusually large, long snake. He was delighted with his find. He played with it for a good while and then called my mother to see his catch. My mother was also impressed with the size of this snake; she called our next door neighbor, Mr. Vanzee, to come take a look. Mr. Vanzee did not have children and he was not very patient with them either. Walking up to our little huddle he began to shout at all of us. He must have had excellent eye sight because even from the distance he was able to identify this snake as a diamond back rattle snake. Quickly Mr. Vanzee moved in and killed the snake.

I don't recall how in the world the local newspaper got involved. However, the next day my brother's picture was plastered over the morning news holding up the great, long rattle snake. Though we were not fans of our neighbor Mr. Vanzee, we were thankful for both his sight and insight. Without his help, we could have been reading a very different story in that morning paper. Mr. Vanzee had saved us that day. Maybe his picture should have been in the paper?

Now we are all grown up and still sometimes we are dealing with snakes. Oh no, not the kind that we caught as children. The snakes of adulthood look friendly enough but they are not. The Bible identifies some of the varieties of these snakes in the following text:

"Now the doings of the flesh are clear; they are immorality, impurity, indecency, idolatry, sorcery, enmity, strife, jealousy, anger (ill temper), selfishness, divisions (dissension's), party spirit, envy, drunkenness, carousing and the like. I warn you beforehand just as I did previously, that those who do such things shall not inherit the kingdom of God" (Galatians 5:19-21).

Just as that old rattle snake looked interesting and fun in the beginning, so these things also look interesting and fun in the beginning as well. In the end of both situations provide the same outcome- death.

God often provides someone like Mr. Vanzee to teach us not to take these serpents by the tail. We often don't like the Mr. Vanzees of life telling us what to do. Who do they think they are anyway? The truth is that these people are trying to save us. Jesus is a little different from Mr. Vanzee. Jesus is patient and He is also able to kill the snakes that we get a hold of before the snakes have the hold on us. Like Mr. Vanzee, Jesus does not come to us until we call out to him.

We didn't catch anymore rattle snakes at our house. Instead, we got some more long lectures on snake catching from our dad. The Father is trying to get us all out of the snake catching business teaching us daily we have no business playing with snakes.

Puzzled

As of this writing, the newspapers have been filled with economic decline, doom and gloom. For some people this news is depressing. Without sounding glib, perhaps that is why the period of economic decline in the 30s was called The Great Depression. Still, there are others who are daily trying to figure out where we are headed and are just plain puzzled by economic events.

When I was a child, I always knew when Christmas was coming. No, it wasn't the trees, toys or the smell of cookies. In fact, it was in "those days" that "those things" did not appear in October or November. Those items usually didn't come out until December 24th. So, it was instead about three weeks before Christmas that my father set up a card table and laid out all the pieces of an intricate puzzle. He did this every year, and to me the puzzle not only meant evenings of fun but that Christmas was on the way.

There were always the "rules" to follow when putting together the family puzzle. One rule was that you were not allowed to force any piece into place. This of course would destroy the piece and ruin the puzzle. Another rule was that we were to collect all the edge pieces and put them together first. One more rule was that we would take all the remaining pieces and sort them by color. Lastly, every evening we would search the floor to be sure we had not dropped or lost a single piece as every piece was needed for the completion of the puzzle.

While I enjoy the memories of that puzzle it makes me think that the puzzle of life is so similar to the workings of the family puzzle. We often have events that don't seem to make since when we only see them in the perspective of the moment they occur. It is the edges that give us the guidelines to begin to build the puzzle. It is the Word of God that provides the boundaries in our lives. It is important not to try to force God into our mold just as the puzzler does not force pieces into places where they don't belong. It is also important to collect the pieces of color that bring out the beauty of the puzzle. There is an importance to each piece even if it alone does not look important.

Just before Christmas, we would finish the puzzle. We would all admire the lovely picture that we were not able to see until the puzzle was completed. The table with our puzzle would be left out during the Christmas season and I recall all those nice comments about all the labor invested and how it was all worth it in the end.

I John 3:2 says:

"Beloved, now we are children of God and it has not yet been revealed what we shall be, but we know that when He is revealed we shall be like Him, for we shall see Him as He is. And everyone who has this hope in Him purifies himself, just as He is pure."

One day God will be finished with the puzzle He is creating and completing in our lives. Though some pieces may look gray and dismal at the moment, they will be perfect in their places when the "puzzle" of your life is completed. Then we will all stand in awe and wonder perhaps with comment about how it was all worth the labor invested and finished beauty in the end.

PC

PC could stand for any number of things. It could represent Pre Christ. It could be Post Christ.

It could be Power Control. Today, however, it stands for something that is very offensive to those who hold to traditional values, "political correctness."

This type of PC came into vogue during the last thirty years or so, and it stands against any speech, thought, or action that could possibly offend anyone about anything. Political correctness is not new. It can be traced back to Mao's "Little Red Book." This fact alone should tell us something. Adopted in the 1960s by the radical left in America, today PC is used to silence all those who would stand for upholding traditional values with a historical view of the founding of our country. PC stands for so-called tolerance except for those who would not yield to PC ideology.

I first heard of PC during the early 70s when I was in high school. We were reminded that should we decide to pray at any school event that we must leave out the name of Jesus least we offend anyone. So, all prayers were ended with "in your name." This thinking slowly made its way into all other events where people were gathered and chose to open or close the event with prayer. When my children got to high school thirty years later, PC was used to explain why no prayer in schools would be allowed at all. As a result, even today when Christians gather in their own homes or churches they have a tendency to leave out the name of Christ when they conclude a prayer.

Is leaving out the name of Jesus in prayer really a big deal? You bet. Why do you suppose the enemy wants us to leave out the name of Jesus? When Peter and John prayed for the lame man in Acts 3:6 they said, "silver and gold have I none, but such as I have give I thee, in the name of Jesus Christ of Nazareth rise up and walk." Apparently they knew the power that comes with the name of Jesus.

Acts 4:18 says, "They commanded them not to speak or teach in the name of Jesus." That sounds a little like Mao to me. It looks like even our opposition knows the power of His name.

Acts 4:30 says even more, ". . . and that signs and wonders may be done by the name of the holy child, Jesus."

Does PC stand for power control? You bet. Was PC pre-Christ? Of course it was. Is PC post- Christ? Yes, in fact it is the devil's attempt to erase the name Jesus and His power from all of us.

Is PC politically correct? No way! There is nothing correct about limiting political speech or thought in a free society.

Spiritually, I need every drop of power that God has provided for me. How about you?

I want to ask His blessings upon me, my children and others. How about you?

I desire to see the work of God in this dark and desperate world. How about you?

Start today when you pray. Bow your head and say:

Lord, we have been deceived.
Other men we have believed.
When they told us to take your Name away,
They taught us another way to pray.

And now by grace we can see,
The power meant for us will be,
Used to win the world for thee,
as we say the name of JESUS.

Seven

When we were raising our little ones, we initially took on every possible issue seeking to be the best parents possible. After the exhaustion of trying to fight every battle we finally realized that one had to be selective and choose only the important battles to prevent battle fatigue. I am sure our children were thankful that we had abolished the extreme parenting approach and ended up enjoying our children for the blessing they were and correcting them only when they really needed it.

God is like this. He does not have endless lists of criticisms or demands of perfection for His children. He at the same time is not a permissive parent either. God saves the strong correction for the big issues. There are, in fact, six things that God hates and one more that is an abomination to Him on His "really big list."

"A proud look, a lying tongue, hands that shed innocent blood, a heart that devises wicked plans, feet that are swift in running to evil, a false witness who speaks lies, and one who sows discord among brethren,"
(Proverbs 6:17-19).

Hate is a very strong word. Hate means to loathe, despise, detest and more. So, this list of seven behaviors is no list of minor suggestions. This is a list of absolutes from God saying, "You had better not!" As a mother when I gave my children the word, "you had better not," you better believe I was dead serious and punishment was swiftly following an infraction in any one of those areas.

With that in mind let's then take one more look at the deadly seven.

- A proud look - this is when someone thinks more highly of themselves and less highly of others.
- A lying tongue - to lie, to deceive, to be false in speech for the sake of personal gain.
- Shedding innocent blood - what is more innocent than an unborn child?
- A heart that devises wicked plans – the schemer who always seeks to come against good things.
- Feet that run quickly to evil - this is when we care more for fun than being obedient to the Word of God.
- A false witness who speaks lies - repetition is the key to all learning and God is taking the opportunity to tell us twice that He is completely opposed to lying.
- One who sows discord - Discordia was the Roman Goddess of Strife. She was the author of relational division and the one who plants the seeds of division within the body of Christ has crossed the heavenly line and is a war with God Himself.

Our heavenly Father takes no joy in bringing us down a peg or two to teach us humility. He loves to bless us. So, today when you go on your way, keep God's directives in your mind and leave those seven deadly stinkers behind.

18,000,000

If numbers count for anything, then eighteen million should count for something. According to a recent study there are eighteen million alcoholics in America. Are you amazed? I sure was, and it made me remember a story.

When I was a young girl, my father had great disdain for his sister. She had made some poor choices in her life. One of those poor choices was taking the road to alcoholism. My father loved her deeply and even went out to bars at times to make sure she got home safely. Later, I heard the conversations when he got home. He spoke of his disgust for her and her choices.

It was about 25 years later that my brothers and I were faced with confronting our own father with his alcoholism. This was a man who never thought he could become a lowly alcoholic. My parents were in the habit of a glass of wine here and there or a drink after a hard day. They were very sure of themselves that they could handle social drinking without it becoming a problem. They were both very wrong and each suffered in their own way because of the hold alcohol had on their lives.

My father had tremendous will power. His strength of will and determination was more than in any other person I had ever met. Yet, his will was not sufficient to save him when the drink had him instead of him having the drink. Will power alone is not sufficient to save eighteen million other Americans either suffering from the bondage of alcoholism.

Proverbs 20:1 says:

"Wine is a mocker, Strong drink is a brawler, and whoever is led astray by it is not wise."

Eighteen million Americans never believed that the first drink could lead them to misery but it did.

So be wise, take care, and do not be led astray.
Take a little lesson from God's word today!
Do not be mocked by a little wine
Keep instead a sober mind.

Take the lesson, add up the cost
Think of all the lives that have been lost
Or countless suffering of so many others
Fathers, Sisters, Mothers, Brothers...

Wishing they could turn back the time
And refuse when offered that first glass of wine.

S.T.A.R.

During the early days of raising our children, we noticed one particular thing about the nature of kids - they want what they want and they want it now. I'm not really sure, but I am convinced this phenomenon pertains to all children. After all, we who are adults have our own wants, and according to a national study, the average person (adult that is) is carrying quite a debt load on credit cards to prove this hypothesis.

This all adds up to one thing — impulse! Impulsive behavior could get a kid in a lot of trouble.

Impulse buying (eating, wrath, etc.) can also get a big kid in another kind of trouble. Impulse means a sudden, spontaneous, inclination or urge. We have all felt and dealt with those urges.

As parents, we realized with three little ones, we were not fast enough to counteract every urge in time to avoid dangers to our children. So, my husband came up with a little teaching tool to help our children reconsider their actions before they acted. We later discovered this acrostic was included in a research study regarding standardized exams. This mental tool to control impulse behavior is called S.T.A.R.

S - Stop
T - Think
A – Act
R - Review your actions.

When we were out in public and we saw one of our little ones about to urge forward into trouble we would just say "STAR." The child would instantly stop and give consideration to any following action. The child was not embarrassed by public shame because no one but our family understood the command. This tool was not only a blessing to us as weary parents but it was a great tool to apply to our own behavior and urges as well.

Proverbs 14:29 says,". . . but he who is *impulsive* exalts folly."

Today you may need a little "STAR" to help you control your own impulses. Try it and see if you do not have a better day and fewer charges on your credit card too!

Snakes in the Grass

I was out working in the yard and trimming shrubbery. It was just that time of year to get these things done. While I was working, I noticed an area where the shrubbery had grown up to the house. Knowing that this is not good for the house, I slowly made my way behind the bush and proceeded to clean a clear path between the bush and the house.

The bush was about chest high and quite deep. As I continued to work, I heard a noise that I was not accustomed to hearing. Against my better judgment, I continued to work and I ignored the noise. This was not a good idea. Within a few more minutes, I discovered a large snake looped in the branches of the bush!

Needless to say, I quickly removed myself from the bushy area. When I recovered my wits, I also reconsidered my steps. I had been keeping an eye on where I was stepping thinking that snakes are usually found on the ground. I also was aware that snakes like bushy areas and was trying to be careful. The one thing I forgot to do was pay attention to the sounds I was hearing. I failed to listen. The moment I heard that rattle I should have been on the run.

The Bible says in Proverbs 9:32-34:

"Now therefore, <u>listen</u> to me, my children,
For blessed are those who keep my ways,
Hear instruction and be wise,
And do not disdain it.
Blessed is the man who <u>listens</u> to me."

Good listening is a seldom practiced art, but my day with that snake has proven to increase my desire to listen well. I find myself very thankful that God protected me from the snake! As, I had failed to listen to the warning that was meant to protect me. It seems so easy to do things our own way, but "the end thereof may be death."

Snakes can be anywhere not only on the ground. They may not be where we often expect to find them. The final lesson we can learn is that all the snakes in life are not of the slithering reptile variety. Snakes are those things and even people who silently linger in the bush to attack us when we are not paying attention.

Today, listen to The Word of God! Let those snakes alone and let them pass because all the snakes of life are not in the grass.

Dance Steps

Slow, slow, quick, quick - dance steps are not easy to learn! They must be taken in the correct order to produce the lovely dance that they were intended to produce. In my first attempt to fox trot, I was ready to trot right out of the class. My instructor had all the right moves, but my feet seemed to have other ideas. At moments, my mind seemed to have all the right steps in sequence until my feet hit the floor and someone's toes took the punishment. The key to learning to dance was to tell my feet what they would do and do it over and over and over again until I had those feet under my control.

The next dance was the ballet. This dance involves so much more than just your feet. Other parts of my body were put under extreme discipline and repetitive motions. Yet, in the end, the ballet was worth the work it took to learn it. One thing I do know about ballet is that it is never completely learned. Ballet is a lifelong discipline.

There are many different "dances" in our Christian walk. There is the dance of devotion to God.

There is the dance of relationship to others. There is the dance of our relationship with this world and all that it treasurers. This list could go on and on. One dance worth discussing is the dance of listening.

Perhaps you have been in a conversation with someone and before they finish their comment you have an answer or reply. This is a missed step! Conversation and communication requires both listening and speaking. So, if you are thinking about your response before you allow the other person to finish their comment you are not communicating with anyone but yourself.

This type of step only works with ballet. Ballet can be performed alone, but it really is so much better to see the whole troop of dancers work together. Listening well to another person first requires that we care about the person and what they have to say. Like dancing, it might take some time to slow down and think about the person before you think about your own response. In the end, you will be far more effective in this partnership of listening just like a good dance pair works the dance floor with fluid harmony and in the end no one's toes will suffer for it.

The One that Got Away

"..And he sins who hastens with his feet"
Proverbs 19:2

The biggest fish stories are about the fish that never ended up in a net. These stories provide some entertainment around a camp fire and quite a number of laughs in future telling of the "fish story," but it isn't very funny when the fish in the story is not a fish at all.

What fish is not a fish? It is the one the salesman caught when you have bought what you should not. The salesman angler knows his bait such as, "buy it now or it will be too late," or "this is the last one in stock." There are a number of these bait lines that gets you caught. Here is a good one – "have I got a deal I have for you." The deal ends up providing you bills with payments due that you cannot afford.

No, the smart fish seeing the bait takes it slow,
Remembering other fish he used to know.
Who snatched the bait that looked so tasty,
And got caught on a hook while being hasty.

Today let there be no regrets,
Be the sort of fish who avoids the net.
The sort of deals that get away,
Are ones God never intended any way.

Go slow little fish,
Don't end up in a pot,
Like the silly fish who would not,
Slow down, and think, wait and pray,
To avoid a trap of debt to pay.

Someday you'll be the story of the big fish in the lake,
That no one could catch on any bait.
And the little minnows will be watching you,
To learn the wisdom for life that has proved true.

Leave others with regrets the bills to pay,
While you be the fish that got away.

Alex

"He who walks with wise men will be wise,
But the companion of fools will be destroyed."
Proverbs 13:20

There are all kinds of sayings that teach us to take care when we choose our companions.

My father would often quote a familiar piece of sage wisdom, "If you lay down with dogs you will get up with fleas." My mother was fond of saying, "One rotten apple can ruin the whole barrel." When training my own children, I would frequently remind them, "Bad company corrupts good morals."

With all these wise sayings to guide them, you would think my children would have made all the right decisions when choosing their friends. Unfortunately, this was not always the case. They had a different saying all together! They would say, "I will just enjoy being with these kids and they won't have any effect on me." This was very frustrating to me, as the last thing a mother wants to see is her children suffer consequences from bad choices.

One day Alex came to play. Alex was eight and his behavior was never great! His parents adopted the saying, "Oh, boys will be boys." This attitude left the rest of the parents in our neighborhood shaking in their boots with what Alex could come up with next.

One day, I was only standing about ten feet away watching Alex and my son start to play. They seemed to be innocently tossing stones in the brook. Then my mother instinct told me to take a close look. As I approached them, I discovered they were actually throwing the stones at a hornets' nest. Before I could stop them they made a direct hit on the nest and ran to escape the ensuing furry of the angry little creatures.

Flying in furry, the hornets were all over my little boy stinging him everywhere!

Thank God my husband came driving up the street getting home early from work. What a sight to greet him with a sobbing little boy still wearing the remains of dead hornets on his body. He grabbed our son, who had taken the brunt of the attack, and made the run for the emergency room.

Now I am sure that Alex was not completely to blame. After all, my son was old enough to make his own choices. It hardly seemed fair that somehow, Alex escaped without a single sting that afternoon, while our boy spent his afternoon in the hospital.

The end is just like the beginning. You will become exactly like the company you keep. The wise becomes wiser and the fools become weak.

The Yellow Brick Road

I n the movie, "The Wizard of Oz," Dorothy and her friends were on a quest to find The Emerald City. The great and notable wizard lived there, and it was his help that Dorothy needed to find her way home to Kansas.

Dorothy was new to Oz and to find her way to the wizard she was told that she must **follow the yellow brick road.** In an effort to be sure that she would stay on course and reach her destination, Dorothy and her friends even sang about following that yellow brick road.

Often we are just like Dorothy. Some truths are new to us in the same way that Dorothy was new to Oz. At those times, we need to reach for the map to find our way and safely arrive at our destination. The Bible is a sure map for the road of life, yet sometimes the words used in even the easiest versions are not the words we use in everyday life. So, just reading the words without understanding can cause a person to miss a much needed directions to travel this path through life.

Here is an example. Proverbs 21:24 states, "A proud and haughty man — Scoffer is his name;

He acts with arrogant pride."

I am glad that the Bible tells us a little about Mr. Scoffer. I also must admit that *scoffer* is not a word used in my daily language. So, it is easy to skip over what I do not know and not be on the lookout for this guy. In fact, without the information, I might even be this guy.

Scoffer is found eleven times in the New King James Version of the Bible. If we follow that road each verse tells us one more thing about his character. Let's begin with the word and follow the road of definition to see what this fellow is about.

Scoff or Scoffer: One who will mock or treat with derision. I also don't ordinarily use the word *derision,* so let's continue our study with that word.

Derision: to act contemptuous or ridicule. This gets us a little closer to the root meaning, but again I must admit that I also don't usually use the word *contemptuous.*

Contemptuous: to show a lack of respect, or to despise, or to show a lack of reverence; to show open disrespect. Now we are getting close!

By definition, Mr. Scoffer is the guy who shows disrespect to others, he despises and hates, he is irreverent and disrespectful. The Bible says in the above verse that he is proud and arrogant. Now we are seeing the picture. He is one of the big sink holes on the road to a fulfilled life.

When God warns us about something or someone, it is important to follow the road of understanding to see what in the world God thinks is so important. God seeks to inform us through His Word. God is far better than a wizard and the Bible more than a city of promise. As sure as Dorothy eventually got home by what she already had with her, you too will find your way to the lesson by following what you already have with you that is the Bible. And by the way, watch out for the scoffer on your trip.

Rise Again

Popeye the Sailor, a popular cartoon character, used to say, "Well, blow me down," during times when he was either perplexed or overcome by life circumstances. I like that statement. The meaning I get from this remark is that sometimes there are events that are beyond my strength or over my head. This is often the case with trials of various types.

Sometimes a circumstance may knock you down. Once you are down, it might be in the back of your mind - "I wonder if I will recover from this one?" Here is the absolute answer to that question. "For a righteous man may fall seven times and rise again, but the wicked shall fall by calamity." Proverbs 24:16

Righteous just means those who choose to go the "right way."

Wicked needs no definition, and calamity has an interesting meaning - it means terrible loss, lasting distress, and adding afflictions.

Life will be filled with ups and downs. For Christians going God's way, all those ups and downs will be used for good in their lives, and they will recover and recover over and over again.

The wicked will have ups and downs of their own, but they will suffer terrible loss, lasting distress, and added afflictions.

When Popeye said, "Blow me down," he would just shake his head and walk off. When I say "blow me down" it means it is time to kneel down and wait to rise again.

Merry Christmas

The weather was getting cooler and the stores had begun to decorate for the Christmas. The smells of gingerbread and other Christmas goodies were beginning to fill our home. I was twelve-years-old and like all children I was getting excited about Christmas. Our home was not a Christian home, so the thing I enjoyed most about the season was all the lovely gifts that we would open on Christmas Eve.

Even at twelve I still was a firm believer in Santa Claus. I was always bubbling over with enthusiasm as the days drew nearer and nearer to the 25th of December. I would babble on and on about Santa during the daily countdown too.

With hind sight, now I can see that I was driving my middle brother to the limits of his tolerance level. Finally the moment came when he could take it no longer. He grabbed my hand and said "I'll show you Santa!" Then he lead me to my parents bedroom (where no children were ever allowed), opened my mother's closet, and pointed to the piles of pretty wrapped gifts stacked in the corner. "There is your Santa!" he proclaimed.

Crushed, I could only stare and thought there must be some mistake. These gifts surely would be for something else. My brother was aware of my unbelief and quickly added, "If you don't believe it now, then you sure will Christmas morning." Ah, the boy was right. Christmas morning arrived and there were those gifts all with tags saying, "From Santa." The dream was over and the doors to childhood-make-believe had forever closed with a crushing thud.

Some things are just better left alone. Some dreams of make believe will dissipate on their own.

Knowing more is not always good for us. Sometimes we learn more than we should. God does not always tell us everything. Proverbs 25:2 says: "It is the glory of God to conceal a matter."

Even now, as an adult, I often wonder about things that I don't understand. Some doors God has left closed to me until the time that I am prepared to receive more knowledge. Hind sight gave me mercy for my brother and his exasperation with me. Hind sight gives me gratitude to God for the information that would have caused me suffering if God had given it to me to early.

What about Santa and childhood dreaming?
Are these just the works of big business scheming?
Can these things have any benefit to the season?
Can they come to grips with right and reason?
Can they add to a child some temporal joy?
For Christ, Himself was once a boy.

This year when you celebrate Christ in Christmas, may you indulge in a few childhood joys, sample cookies, and buy a few toys. Share your table and goodies with family and friends. It is God's gift of love that Christmas sends. Merry Christmas.

Jokes

"Like a madman who throws firebrands, arrows and death, so is the man who deceives his neighbor, and says, **'I was only joking!'**" Proverbs 26:18-19.

Most of us as children heard the rhyme, "sticks and stones may break my bones but, names will never hurt me." While I know the rhyme, I do not know the author. Perhaps it was a mother who in earnest hoped the words of others would do less damage when placed in the light of this little rhyme.

Oh, words do hurt. Words not only ring out in the moment that they come out, they seem to revive many times throughout our lives. With each resounding memory, the pain that they deliver again echoes in memory — even when the child moves into adulthood.

In my experience as a pastor's wife, I have met more people who have experienced this pain than you might imagine. It seems that when someone is hurt in this manner, they also tend to believe that they alone are suffering this type of hurt. This is untrue and isolating. My experience is that 100% of the people I know have been on the rotten end of hurtful words at one time or another.

Now you might think that if a person had suffered from hurtful words they certainly would never deliver such blows to others. This is not true either but shocking that those who have been hurt by wounding words would do the same thing to someone else. It is also convicting to the person who suddenly realizes that they have delivered a wound to another.

In that second, many times an individual may say, "Oh, I was only joking," in a lame attempt to cover their tracks. Again - not true! Jokes are to be amusing or fun remarks. Hurtful comments are not jokes. When seeing we have said the wrong thing it is only right to admit the fault and seek the forgiveness from the one who was hurt.

Proverbs is so clear and much stronger than I can begin to match in expressing the poor character in a person who indulges in a lack of self control with their mouth. It says they are like madmen, throwing arrows and firebrands (pieces of burning wood) and death at others.

Words seem to remain and cause others tears, grief and pain.
They pierce like arrows and wound the heart,
Making jokes of folks with the ache they impart.

Today is a great day to be more careful with what we say!

Horn Blowing

The blowing of horns, such as a trumpet, a shofar, or a bugle has played important roles in history. These instruments signaled both victory and alarm. They pronounced a time of assembly and also a call to faith. They signal the start of a day for some and signal evening for others. They play to entertain us and they play to close the funeral for those who have fallen in service to the nation.

During our years in the military, each morning we woke to the sound of the bugle call for Reveille. Funny how, even though it came early in our day, it was still a welcome sound to the Army family. In the evening we would hear Retreat and "To the Colors" played as the flag was lowered. At this time, every person stopped in their tracks, every car was required to stop, and then every person would stand and turn toward our flag and salute as it lowered for the night. Once the flag was down each person continued on their way, but for a few moments we had all shared a tribute to Old Glory.

A flag cannot honor itself. It is honored because of what it represents to us. People, like a flag, should not brag, boast or endeavor to honor themselves. Real honor is bestowed when it comes from the mouth of another celebrating and extolling behavior that is exemplary.

Proverbs 27:2 says:

"Let another man praise you and not your own mouth,
A stranger, and not your own lips."

When I was very little girl, I heard my father talk about someone, "blowing their own horn."

I asked him what he meant thinking someone was playing some kind of music. My dad said how it was just poor character to brag on yourself, and in fact, it made other people think poorly of you.

Praise always sounds so sweet when it comes to those who do not seek it. One should not waste their time on the "praise" when they think they are due it. Rather we all should seek to praise others for what they have done for us. When it comes to bugle blowing, one should think of what their lives are showing and modeling to make difference for others and not their own glory.

Every year we take the time to honor those who have given of their time, talent, and service to our country by way of military service. This week let's honor those who honored us all by giving their lives to serve and protect us. Let's take a moment or two and offer to them and to God the praise that is due. One thing is certain; you will never catch them blowing their own horns.

The Higher Road

Daniel faced a set of circumstances as bad and challenging as any of us could imagine. No doubt his family was killed when he was taken captive to Babylon. For reasons known only to God, he was kept alive to serve in the court of King Nebuchadnezzar. Daniel was most probably a young teenager, but his response to his circumstances was hardly those of an ordinary teen. He demonstrates in his response to his trials how to live a life of peace during the worst storms that can come.

You may wonder, "What were the trials and storms in the life of Daniel?" First, there was death as many were killed during the destruction of Jerusalem in 606 B.C. Second, he was taken captive to serve the very people responsible for the destruction of his country, family, and friends. Here was the temptation for self pity and bitterness, yet Daniel chose rather to believe and trust in God.

Third, Daniel needed patiently to wait three years in the court of the eunuchs to prepare for what God had for Him. Waiting can be a very difficult challenge for us while we are trusting God to reveal His plan and purpose for our lives. The king thought that this training was to serve him; however, this training was preparing Daniel to serve the Lord.

The fourth struggle came for Daniel when he had to choose to resist the temptation of going along with the crowd. It seems that Daniel decided to keep himself from things that would defile him, so he gave up the goodies of Babylon to eat vegetables — that was quite a decision for a young man.

I would sum up Daniel's choices like this:

Dedication: he dedicated his life to God

Separation: he choose to separate himself from the things of this world

Preparation: he was willing to wait three years preparing for what God had for him

Cooperation: he then was ready to cooperate with God in ministry.

We can all be like Daniel, but only we can choose the higher road. This is neither the quick trip, nor the easy one either. Let's not forget the end of Daniel's story - from the sorrow of loss and captivity to the right hand of the king. I would say it was worth it — how about you?

Suit Up

It is apparent to me today, that God is about to use our little church and those who love Him for a specific purpose. Whether we become soldiers in the military or soldiers of the cross, it is necessary for those who serve, to "suit up" for battle. In the case of believers, the victory is assured. Wouldn't every soldier like those odds?

I Peter 3:15 gives us the needed charge for today when it states ". . . always be ready to give a defense to everyone who asks you a reason for the hope that is in you, with meekness and fear."

For some time now, you have been "storing up" God's Word in your hearts never knowing exactly what His plan of action was going to be for you. Even now you may be waiting for your call to battle not knowing when you might receive that call.

In times past, the shofar would sound and Israel would rally and ready their soldiers for the war. One young soldier once told me he was excited to finally be deployed to the desert. Frankly, I thought he was nuts. However, as our conversation continued, he explained that this was what his training was for and he knew in his heart that he was ready for action. This young man wanted to be "the difference." He wanted to stand up and answer his country's call to arms because he was already "suited up" for war.

As the Lord continues to open our eyes and reveal His plan of action, let all of us be ready to get up, stand tall and "suit up" for action.

When Great Men Fall

The Book of Daniel, chapter four, begins with Nebuchadnezzar, the king, giving praise and honor to God. He also extols God for the kindness that God had given him and how God had worked in his life. How could a man with such a good beginning turn out to end so poorly?

Within just a few more verses, we find Nebuchadnezzar seeking Daniel's assistance in understanding a dream. In this dream, there was a very strong warning from God that Nebuchadnezzar must not allow pride to dominate his life. With this warning, God also told Nebuchadnezzar what He would do to him if he took God's glory for himself. In the face of such a strong consequences Daniel tells the king the only logical and reasonable thing to do.

"Therefore, O king, let my advice be acceptable to you; break off your sins by being righteous, and your iniquities by showing mercy to the poor, Perhaps there may be a lengthening of your prosperity" Daniel 4:27.

This was great advice to a great man, but Nebuchadnezzar did not take the advice.

"At the end of twelve months he was walking about the royal palace of Babylon. The king spoke, saying, 'Is not this great Babylon that I have built for a royal dwelling by my mighty powers and for the honor of my majesty?'" Daniel 4: 29-30.

The chapter goes on to tell us that while the words were still in his mouth, the king became like a wild ox. For seven years he roamed and lived as an animal. He did this until he had a change of heart and gave God glory for his blessings. Every great man can learn from the king of the greatest kingdom on earth. The lesson is to forsake the temptation to take God's glory and take credit for His great works and many blessings.

Many years ago, my husband had an employer who told him, "you do all the work, and I get all the credit for it." Now any employee would find this difficult to take. In a few years, we moved on to a new duty station and a new boss and were looking forward to new thinking. It seems that the mindset of the old boss was not unusual and popped up many times during my husband's career. Perhaps not all the Nebuchadnezzar's are dead in Babylon.

No matter what your status, the temptation to take credit instead of giving credit is a dangerous temptation. Today, take a lesson from Daniel.

When pride comes knocking,
Don't answer the door.
We have Nebuchadnezzar's example,
We don't need one more.

Holiday Turkey

The savory smells of Thanksgiving trigger many blessings for which we can be truly grateful. In our house, it takes about two full days of preparations for the "Thanksgiving Day Feast." Afterward, it takes about a month of exercise to pay for the added weight that comes with it.

My grandson, Connor, says it best — "yummy, yummy, yummy!" The rest of us just nod and smile because we all agree with him. Few things are as welcome or as wonderful, as the holiday meal and our family all gathered together and the dining table.

Turkey preparations are not difficult for the cook, but there are a few rules to follow for the safe handling of poultry. There are of course, thawing instructions, baking instructions, stuffing instructions, and carving instructions. Between all of these instructional moments, there is the most important rule — wash your hands and everything else the raw turkey comes into contact with during the cooking process. When cooks follow these rules, the meal will not only be a tasty delight but free of contamination as well.

The turkey serves as the center piece of the feast, but is not enough to provide an entire meal. In fact, whenever families gather there are many side dishes to sample. One such side dish is most important. It is the dish of kindness and compassion. People, like turkeys, require safe handling too. Turkeys can carry germs and require hand washing. People carry their own "contaminates by way of their faults that will require undeserved love and mercy in order for the family to enjoy being together.

A slang name for germs is bugs, and what bugs you about one person may not be the same thing that "bugs" someone else. In fact, your own "bugs" may bug others more than you think. The only alternative to loving people when they do not deserve your love is to isolate yourself from people and be lonely, miserable, and eat your turkey by yourself.

I John 4:7 says:

"Love one another; for love is of God; he who loves is born of God and knows God. He who does not love does not know God, for God is Love."

I believe this verse gives us a very good reason to let the turkey in the oven be the only turkey we roast during a holiday season. Bon appétit!

Falling Leaves

During the fall season, the leaves are falling crisp and brown from the trees that were recently full of lush green foliage. It seems hard to believe that only a few weeks into fall, the cooler temperatures will bring the season into focus as you reach for your wool coat.

It looks like our economic season is falling suit. Once we were nationally "in the money" and yet even this week our leadership has announced that we are in an official recession.

Just like fall, it happened while we slept. The cooler evening temperatures brought down the leaves as the chill was just too much for the trees to maintain them. In that same way, consumer confidence has also fallen while we were lulled to sleep by poor judgment and our personal and national sins that have finally chilled our poor, ailing economy.

The Bible tells us of other nations who made similar poor choices and had to endure their own fall from the top. Daniel 9:13 does a perfect job of teaching us what to do during such a season - ". . . all this disaster has come upon us; yet we have not made our prayer before the Lord our God, that we might turn from our iniquities and understand Your truth."

The seasons of the year come and go according to a set time. The seasons of decline for man are dependent on a change of heart, and the prayer of a repentant people that will lead to a repentant nation. This type of fall only will last as long as it takes to affect the change that God is seeking to make within us. Daniel 9:19 gives us just such a prayer to teach us how to repent.

"O Lord, hear!
O Lord, forgive!
O Lord, listen and act!
Do not delay for Your own sake.
My people are called by Your name."

One more glance at the falling leaves reminds me that though winter is on the way, that it is also in the winter that we celebrate the joy of Christmas. Isn't that interesting? When life is most cold, it is then that we truly celebrate the Savior.

May the leaves we see falling teach us today,
To fall on our knees to seek God and to pray.
Let us learn to repent and show others the way,
As our lives demonstrate the words that we say!

I pray today as I see the leaves falling, that the trees of our lives will never be brown, withered or dry. I know God hears a repentant soul's cry. He will restore us again as we make new choices, pray, and leave fall to the leaves that cool winds drive away.

An Icy Blast

As I looked out over the park, I saw the effects of our first real winter blast. It's only fall, but winter does not always abide by nor accommodate the almanac and calendar. The grass was frozen so solid that it was sticking up like a million frosted spikes. The remainder of neglected leaves clung to one another in a frozen array welded to the trunks of the trees.

My neighbors, the ones brave enough to get out and walk, were bundled up from the top of their heads to the tips of their toes. It is on days like this that I think of staying right in my warm house, with my warm tea, and laying aside my "to do list" for at least one day. However, schedules, like calendars, do not always accommodate a little winter blast.

Daniel felt a chill of another sort during the reign of Cyrus, the king of Persia. He was frozen with fear over what he saw coming in the near and far future of the world. Following days of fasting, he was sitting by the Tigris River when he was given a visitation from The Lord. You might imagine all sorts of things that the Lord could have said to him, but what He said was of such comfort that I cannot even shorten it for this devotion.

"And he said to me, 'O Daniel, man greatly beloved, understand the words that I speak to you, and stand upright, for

I have now been sent to you.' While he was speaking this word to me, I stood trembling. Then he said to me, 'Do not fear, Daniel, for from the first day that you set your heart to understand and to humble yourself before your God, your words were heard; and I have come because of your words.'"
Daniel 10:11-12

What could bring more warmth to the soul than hearing once again that we are greatly loved? What could calm the storms of life more than the encouraging words, "do not fear?" What can melt the icy blast more than knowing that God has heard you? In this type of warmth we can become strong to face the storms all winter long.

Stars that Shine

While preparing for our children's Christmas play, I was working on little star costumes. Though the costumes took time to put together, I enjoyed the process imagining our little ones and how precious they would look in their play. Along with the costumes, we held rehearsals, encouraging them to memorize their lines, reminding them to watch their words, to speak clearly, take cues off of each other, and not to worry about stage fright during the performance. Does any of this sound familiar to you?

God is working on His own play and we are His little stars. You and I are the children who act in the parts He has chosen for us. Our script is the Bible and with that script He coaches us on:

1. Speech - what we say, how we say it, and timing of our words
2. Action - what we do, how we do it, and when He wants it done
3. Interaction - how we treat one another and develop sensitivity to others in the roles they play
4. Stage Fright - that He is always there to help us when stage fright seems to overwhelm us.

At the end of each Christmas play, I always have a little treat for each of the children. You might call it a little blessing or a reward, and they are always thrilled with whatever treat I find to give them. God has promised a treat for His players too.

"Those who are wise shall shine like the brightness of the firmament . . . ."
Daniel 12:3

It seems like I am not the only one working on star costumes! One day very soon we shall all be like the stars that shine.

Seeking a Savior

"Now after Jesus was born in Bethlehem of Judea in the days of Herod the king, behold, wise men from the East came to Jerusalem, saying, 'Where is He who has been born King of the Jews?'"
Matthew 2:1-2

No one really knows how far these wise men traveled. No one knows how many men there were, but the odds are that it was not the traditional three we most often hear about. No one knows what struggles they went through as they journeyed seeking our Savior Jesus. The one thing we do know is that they were well aware of their need to find the King of Kings.

You could say that our world has completely changed from that day long ago. You could say that our cultures and jobs don't even compare to life in ancient times. Our problems seem so complex and our own journeys so different. The one thing I know for sure is that we all still need Jesus.

Even if the problems of our times seem different — they are no problem for a living God. Even if our cultures seem to collide with Biblical thinking - Biblical thinking is still right. Even if the list of things in our lives that need repair seems endless, they are still no match for the eternal God in whom your very breath is.

Today, as you go along your way, be ready to give directions to people still seeking the Savior. Today, as you look at your situations an shake your head, take time to bow and give them to the One who can fix all things according to the plans and purposes He has for your life.

Finally, today might be a good day to remember that the wisdom of those wise men of old guided them to seek the Savior. In the world in which we live today, how wonderful it would be to say, "wise men still seek Him."

O Holy Night

Can you believe that the first music ever to sound over public air waves was "O Holy Night?" Wow, we have come a long way down given what you hear on the radio stations of today.

"O Holy Night" was originally written in French and then translated into English in the early 1900s. There is one line in the song that stands out to me: "*Long lay the world, in sin and error pining.*" The word *pining* is seldom used in our language today. So, when we are singing about *pining*, it would be easy to pass over this word and fail to grasp its meaning.

Pining means to suffer a tense longing for something. Now the words of the song come into focus for us. "*Long lay the world, in sin and error pining (suffering a tense longing for),*" but pining for what? Well the rest of the song tells us, "Until He appeared and the soul found it's worth."

In all the philosophies, all the science, and all the religions of the world, we, as humans, still struggle and yes even pine for meaning, value, and purpose in our lives. We still struggle in search of a conclusive answer to the question, "Why am I here?" Only when we follow the instructions in Matthew 3:2 can we find the answer to our pining; "Repent, for the kingdom of God is at hand!"

The sins and errors of this world keep us separated from our Holy God. When Christ came, His purpose in coming to this world was to pay the price for our sins and errors and reunite us back to God. To receive His forgiveness and begin the process of reconciliation, we are called to "repent."

Repent is a wonderful compound Greek word. *Metanouia* literally means to change your mind. To change your mind about living a self-centered life of pleasure and to surrender to the lordship of Jesus Christ is repentance – to stop going in one direction and turn around in another direction.

When we turn from the hopelessness of going our own way and turn and go God's way, we are reunited to the relationship that gives our lives meaning, value, and purpose. Once we are in proper relationship with God, we are then able to see His will and plan for our lives.

Once there was no hope.
The world was lost in sin.
Until God sent us a Savior,
That drew us back to Him.

Amen?

Like A Child

Working with children is such an interesting ministry. These little people have such an ability to go about their days without the least worry or concern that seem to plague so many adults. Children, it appears, simply enjoy life. They enjoy having fun. They invest so much of their time in playing and laughing. Even the smallest sticker or little treat make their emotions rise and not only do they enjoy these items they spread that joy to others who watch their little smiles.

When I am teaching my class, I seldom have a child try to take over and tell me that I am not in control. Notice I said seldom do I have a child try to take over control. For the most part, the class eagerly waits with looks of anticipation, their expressions speaking, "What are we going to do today Miss Sue? Hey Miss Sue, how are we going to do that?"

Jesus said, "Unless you are converted and become as little children, you will by no means enter the kingdom of heaven" (Matthew 18:3). I believe He was giving us a word picture of trusting Him to be the teacher of our class. Like these little children, we too are to look to Jesus with that expectation of what we are to do and how we are going to do it.

The Bible says we are not supposed to be anxious about tomorrow. Stress is a primary contributor to so many forms of illness. Rather than worry, we are called to live moment by moment, entering into the rest of God, living a life of trust and joy knowing that our Teacher has the class firmly in His control. Today would be a good time to take a lesson from the children.

A New Year's Blessing

You know when it's January. The New Year has come in with celebrations all over the world. Something about the New Year that says we can start over, that everything can be new and fresh. It reminds me of holding a newly minted coin. It is bright, clean, and brand new with no flaws or imperfections.

January is the time to make resolutions, to tighten your budget, to work on your waistline, and to open your Bible. It is the time to get your ledgers straight and take a proper financial accounting of last year. We all share anticipation that the coming year will be better for us than the year that just ended.

Anytime you open the books, accounting is inevitable. My family is full of certified accountants who would tell you that when you check the books, some look good and some do not. Nonetheless, this time of accounting is the time to put away excuses and get down to business, the business of life.

This was the case of a young man who came to Jesus seeking not to secure his financial future but his eternal destiny. In their conversation, noted in The Book of Matthew 19:16-24, they discuss the requirements for salvation and the answer to eternal life.

"If you want to enter into life, keep the commandments." Now this sounds simple until you recognize that no one has ever been able to keep all the commandments. So, is there no hope for salvation? The conversation continues when the young man seeks clarification.

"He said to Him, 'Which ones?' Jesus said, 'You shall not murder, you shall not commit adultery, you shall not steal, you shall not bear false witness, honor your father and your mother, and you shall love your neighbor as yourself.'" I find the answer from this young man to be quite amazing. "All these things I have kept from my youth. What do I still lack?"

How many of us can claim to have kept just this small portion of the commandments and to have done so all our lives? My guess is that none of us would even dare make such a claim as the evidence to refute it would be so readily available. Jesus knows everything about us. He knows every area of our lives that are pleasing to Him and every area that is not pleasing. No excuses or rabbit holes will keep Him from identifying and accounting the reality of our behavior.

"Jesus said to him, 'If you want to be perfect, go sell what you have and give it to the poor and you will have treasure in heaven; and come follow me.'"

Here it is! This young man's area of concern was his possessions and Jesus knew it. Just the same way He knows the master passion of your life that competes for your time and attention with Him. The passage of Scripture finishes this way, "But when the young man heard that saying, he went away sorrowful, for he had great possessions." What heartbreak! Having found the road to life this fellow chose another road. I am sure I don't need to tell you where that road leads.

The accounting work we can do in the beginning of a new year, can lead each of us to face the same options in our own lives – live for self or live for Jesus. We too, need to listen as the Lord speaks to us to unload our own possessions that keep us from walking in complete submission to His will for our lives. If you still find that you are not sure of your liabilities, you only need to take another look at verse eighteen. It sure seems to sum it all up. When all the adding and subtracting is done in the light of God's Word, we can see once more our need for a Savior.

May this year be a better one than last,
May your ledgers show profit, not things lost.
May you be brave enough to face the past,
And change your road — no matter the cost.

May your eyes be open,
May you be ready to hear,
The truth of your life,
That only He can make clear.

And when the accounting has all been done,
May He complete in you the work He's begun.

Have a Happy New Year every day!

What's Cooking?

On occasion, I begin preparing our evening meals in the morning. I like to use a Crockpot and slow cook the meal through the course of the day. There is nothing quite like walking into the house, tired from the "do run, run" of the day, and be greeted with the smell of something wonderful in the kitchen upon for your arrival. The same thing happens when you use coffee pots that are preset to come on before you wake up in the morning. As soon as your feet hit the floor, that roasted aroma is calling you to the kitchen.

There is no doubt these modern conveniences have made our lives much easier than in times past when it comes to enjoying the goodies that fill us with pleasure. There is a similar truth that applies to our spiritual appetites as well.

Ephesians 4:25-26 gives us the parallel lesson. "Therefore, putting away lying, let each one of you speak truth with his neighbor, for we are members of one another. Be angry, and do not sin; do not let the sun go down on your wrath, nor give place to the devil."

Just as your evening meal is determined by whatever you have cooking in the pot, so your spiritual life is determined by what you have "cooking" in your heart. Specifically, we are warned not to lie and not to allow either sin or wrath to be slow cooking in our hearts. The Bible warns us not to let the sun set before we get rid of the wrath so it will not develop into worse things that can poison the pot.

We live with the delusion that we can control our behavior so it does not reveal what is really in our hearts. This is simply not true. Just as you eat whatever you have slow cooked all day, so it is with your behavior. Whatever you start with on the inside will reveal itself on the outside. Just as the aroma of the slow cooker is evident to all who enter your house, so too whatever you have in your heart is evident to us as we experience the aroma of your behavior as you interact with others.

The Bible says, "But the fruit of the Spirit is love, joy, peace, long-suffering, kindness, goodness, faithfulness, gentleness, self-control," Galatians 5:22.

Before you speak take time to weigh,
The heart behind the words you say,
For with your speech you will reveal
What is in your pot – just like a meal.

Calvary Chapel of Northeast Columbia was established in 2002 by Pastor Michael E. Frisina and his wife Susan. Their prayer and desire is that the Lord will use this church as a blessing to those who are seeking to grow strong in their faith from the teaching of God's Word and through worship in praise to the Lord. Pastor Mike's vision for the church is to build a healthy, thriving, church body in northeast Columbia that will reach the lost with the saving knowledge of Jesus Christ, and to equip the church body to serve with their spiritual gifts to the glory of the name of Jesus Christ.

Both Pastor Mike and his wife Susan are available for men's, women's, and couple retreats speaking together and separately. For more information on their availability for your conference needs, you can contact them through the church website www.ccnecolumbia.org, email at ccnecolumbia@calvarychapel.com or call 803-865-2586.

LaVergne, TN USA
12 November 2009
163823LV00001B/46/P